# DYING TO LIVE

Other titles in the Discovery Books series

*When All Else Fails . . . Read the Directions*
*Love Story*
*Family Life*
*Authentic Christianity*
*Jesus Teaches on Prayer*
*Spiritual Warfare*
*Understanding Man*
*Behind History*
*Death of a Nation*
*A Nation Under God?*

AN INTRODUCTION TO COUNSELING THAT COUNTS

# DYING TO LIVE

**BOB SMITH**

Discovery Books



**WORD BOOKS, PUBLISHER**
WACO, TEXAS

First Paperback Printing—January 1976
Second Paperback Printing—June 1977
Third Paperback Printing—July 1978



Grateful acknowledgment is made also to the Macmillan Company for permission to quote from *The New Testament in Modern English*, copyright 1958, 1960, 1972 by J. B. Phillips.

DISCOVERY BOOKS are published by Word Books, Publisher, in cooperation with Discovery Foundation, Palo Alto, California.

ISBN 0-87680-883-6

Library of Congress catalog card number: 75-32647

Printed in the United States of America

To the two Mary's: Mary Ann Barnett and Marylou Roe, two faithful women whose initiation and operation of the Compassion Corps at Peninsula Bible Church has conclusively proved the thesis of this book long before it was written. And to all those committed Christians who are engaged in a fruitful counseling ministry—scared, but not scared out of this most necessary aspect of the ministry of the saints, because they keep listening to and trusting the Wonderful Counselor.

*For to us a child is born, to us a son is given; and the government will be upon his shoulder, and his name will be called Wonderful Counselor . . .*

Isaiah 9:6

# CONTENTS

## III. THE THERAPY OF REDEMPTIVE TRUTH

Making men whole (including ourselves) through the application of God's redemptive Word. Dealing with the major issues of life in ways that make life worth living



*And may the God of peace himself fulfill his good purposes in your life to the very end for which he made you, and may your entire being—spirit, soul and body—be kept free of reproach and wholly satisfactory to him in the presence of our Lord Jesus Christ upon his arrival.*

*Faithful is the one calling you, who surely will do it!*

(1 Thessalonians 5:23–24, freely translated)

# FOREWORD

Since World War II we have witnessed a rapidly growing interest in mental health and its many aberrations. The number of people involved in the mental health field has increased to a degree that would have been unthought of thirty years ago. Characteristic of this burgeoning field has been the great variety of theoretical systems proposed as a means to understand and explain poor mental health, or even to deny that poor mental health exists. Methods of evaluation, diagnosis, and treatment are so varied and numerous as to cause some professionals in the mental health field to describe the situation as "chaotic."

Why so many differing and often conflicting theoretical formulations and treatment modalities? The reason is obvious: none have proven themselves, except to their own most subjective adherents, to be clearly and uncontroversially sound. In fact, the opposite is the case! Validation has been highly questionable in every instance due to inconsistent, unpredictable, and unmeasurable results.

Bob Smith, a pastor at Peninsula Bible Church in Palo Alto, California, has had extensive experience in counseling and teaching the principles of counseling as found in God's Word. Here he discusses that "missing dimension" of mental health that has been so ignored and in most instances even denied by the professionals in the present mental health explosion. The "missing dimension" without which true mental health cannot exist!

DR. JOHN C. WAKEFIELD, M.D.
(Practicing psychiatrist in Los Gatos, California, trained in the Menninger School of Psychiatry)

# PREFACE

Everyone's dying to live! But many today are just dying, period. Theirs is the walking death of futility and frustration, the utter boredom and pointlessness of existing without living.

The Lord Jesus said, "I have come that you might have life—the more abundant kind" (John 10:10b). Yet many of us fail to realize the full potential of all that statement means. But the promise of the Lord stands unabridged—waiting only to be claimed by faith. How to achieve some of that fullness of life—for ourselves and others—is the subject of this book.

Our social consciousness of a deeply hurting world is keenly accentuated these days. To do something about it personally is the concern of every Christian heart, I believe—yet how to put in our time and energy where they really count is a common point of frustration for many of us. Our desire in this volume is to suggest some biblical ways we *can* effect healing in the lives we touch, by sharing the redemptive truth of God in a counseling ministry, as part of the ministry of the saints.

The Apostle Paul said to the Corinthians, "So death is at work in us, but life in you" (2 Cor. 4:12). There are two kinds of dying. One, as we have mentioned, is the expression of futility and despair through failure to relate to the one who is to be our *life,* thus missing out on the fullness and fulfillment he gives. The other is dying to one's own ambitions and plans in favor of a better way, God's way, resulting in freedom to be a positive, constructive factor in every situation.

This second kind of dying thus becomes an expression of the *life* of Jesus Christ—for it's the very hallmark of the way he is and does. Could it be we need to die a little—to our own selfish interests and pursuits, so that others who are "dying to live" might *live?*

Dear Brothers—

*If a Christian is overcome by some sin, you who are godly should gently and humbly help him back onto the right path, remembering that next time it might be one of you who is in the wrong. Share each other's troubles and problems, and so obey our Lord's command. If anyone thinks he is too great to stoop to this, he is fooling himself.*

Galatians 6:1–3, *The Living Bible*

## I. A BIBLICAL BASIS OF COUNSELING

Considering the possibilities of Christians really becoming available to God in his business of making men whole.

## CHAPTER ONE

# Comes the Revolution!

Have you ever longed to be a more effective part of that body of Christians who enjoy a consistently redemptive ministry toward this old, bleeding world? There is such a group, you know—God's Compassion Corps, engaged in a wonderfully healing ministry to the many wounded and hurting ones who are all around us today. Their work is the follow-up on our Lord's own ministry to ". . . proclaim release to the captives and recovering of sight to the blind, to set at liberty those who are oppressed . . ." (Luke 4:18).

I believe that it is God's desire for *all* who are Christ's own to engage in this redemptive program. Although it's certainly a privilege to be involved in God's work of healing, that privilege is not reserved for a select few. All Christians are uniquely qualified to be so employed by virtue of the inside information we have about life and the inner fortification we enjoy through the presence of our risen Lord. We shall attempt to document this premise from the Scriptures. It seems, though, that many of us are hesitant to make ourselves available and vulnerable to such a ministry—either because we feel it would be presumptuous to think we are qualified without professional training or because we think it might cost us too much. But the Lord of the church wants us to get over both these hurdles, at least to the point where we can say, "Lord, I'm willing to be convinced—just show me how it's possible. I'm available."

## Counselors Wanted

No one has to be convinced these days that the whole world needs wise counsel. Psychiatrists, psychologists, and marriage and family counselors are doing a booming business.

Has God missed a cue somehow? Is he unaware and uncaring about the widespread human hurt and heartache? Is he deaf to the cries for help and the agony of despair? If you know the God of the Bible and if he is real and reigning, then you know such an idea is unthinkable.

Well, then, have we Christians missed it? I hate to say it, but I think we have. I think we have almost entirely missed God's plan for healing the world's hurts—largely through inattention to his Word on the subject. I say this not to condemn us but to alert us to the potent possibility that we *can* be God's Compassion Corps, and we can undertake this ministry of counseling with confidence.

We have been convinced in our day that counseling is only for the "pros," the psychologists and psychiatrists. Even pastors have been persuaded that counseling is a specialty in which they are largely incompetent—referrals by pastors to professional psychologists are common. If it is true that counseling is for "pros" only, whether psychologists or pastors, it would seem that the ordinary, plain-vanilla Christian has little or no opportunity to be a competent counselor. But if we dare to take seriously what the Bible says on this subject, we come up with a different answer: The counseling ministry is not only for professionals, but *all* Christians should be able to counsel with confidence.

## But Who Qualifies?

When we asked a group of Christians: "Are you competent to counsel?" we got a wide variety of answers. Some thought it was a ridiculous question and didn't even dignify it with an answer; others started to mentally review their college course in psychology.

But one man answered, "I'm not, but Christ is."

What did he mean by that?

Well, knowing him, I think he meant, "By myself I'm not wise enough, but the Lord Jesus who lives in me can supply all I need through his Word and his Spirit to make me adequate."

This may seem far-out, but it's true. The Lord who indwells us is the One whom Isaiah calls, prophetically, "Wonderful Counselor," and he is the *only* one who is truly competent to counsel (see Isa. 9:6). But he makes *us* adequate as we draw on him. This great truth forms the basis of adequacy in any field of endeavor, but it is especially crucial in counseling.

In our Lord's words this truth is stated negatively in John 15:5: "Without me you can do nothing." Positively, it is put before us again in 2 Corinthians 3:5–6: "Not that we are sufficient of ourselves to claim anything as coming from us; our sufficiency is from God, who *has* qualified us to be ministers of a new covenant . . ." Are we qualified to counsel? The answer is: "Yes, as the Lord who lives in us makes us adequate, then we are qualified."

## Revolution

The world view, however, is that counseling belongs in the hands of the professionals. As if to punctuate that idea, a recent headline blares: "NUMBER OF CHILDREN IN U.S. SEEING PSYCHIATRISTS SOARS DRAMATICALLY."

We send even our children to psychiatrists. But in the world of *professionally* qualified counselors—particularly in the field of psychiatry—there is something of a revolution going on. To see what I mean by this, read William Glasser's *Reality Therapy,* from which I would like to quote. (Dr.

Glasser is a psychiatrist, and this is a secular book, not written from a specifically Christian point of view.) Note what O. Hobart Mowrer (also a psychiatrist) says in the foreword to this book:

> For more than a decade now it has been evident that something is seriously amiss in contemporary psychiatry and clinical psychology. Under the sway of Freudian psychoanalysis, these disciplines have not validated themselves either diagnostically or therapeutically. Their practitioners, as persons, have not manifested any exceptional grasp on the virtues and strengths they purportedly help others to acquire. And the impact of their philosophy of life and conception of man and society as a whole has been subtly subversive.

Remember, this is a psychiatrist speaking.

> Because they were the main "losers," laymen were the first to become vocal in their discontent, distrust, and cynicism. But today there is a "shaking of the foundations" in professional circles as well. For example, a state hospital superintendent recently said to me, "Yes, we too think we have a good hospital here. At least we aren't doing the patients any harm. And that is progress." In the past, we psychiatrists have often spread the disease we were supposedly treating.

That, I submit, is quite a confession from someone in the world of psychiatry. That world is in the process of questioning its own premises, and Dr. Glasser has emerged from the "shaking of the foundations" with a new approach to therapy —new, that is, from the standpoint of classical psychiatry. But how new is it, really?

## A New Kind of Therapy—From an Old Book

First of all, as I see it, his basic premise is *responsibility instead of permissiveness.* That indeed is a switch from traditional therapeutic approaches, particularly from modern interpretations and the end results of Freudian approaches.

From this base Dr. Glasser, revealing keen insight, points out some very fundamental needs of humanity. Although this is a secular book, Dr. Glasser points up some things that the Bible has been proclaiming all along.

For instance, he bases his therapy on the fact that *men need to love and be loved.* Does that sound like something you might have discovered in the Bible? He goes from there to the fact that *all of us need to feel a sense of worth;* we need to feel worthwhile to ourselves and to others. As a careful student of human nature, Dr. Glasser has discovered a truth that has been revealed in the Bible but ignored by much of the world for centuries, and he builds his whole approach to counseling on these truths.

To quote *Reality Therapy* again: "At all times in our lives *we must have at least one person who cares about us and for whom we care ourselves.* If we do not have this essential person, we will not be able to fulfill our basic needs" (emphasis mine). With almost no effort, we can fill out Dr. Glasser's insightful words with the truth that we have. Who is he describing? Who is that "essential person"? In my book, his name is Jesus Christ—the one Person who is essential for all of us.

Then Dr. Glasser cites one essential characteristic this person must have: "*He must be in touch with reality* himself and able to fulfill his own needs within the world" (emphasis mine). Who does that describe? Do you know anyone other than our Lord who is fully in touch with reality and who can be completely fulfilled in himself?

Dr. Glasser continues: "Without that key person through whom we gain the strength and encouragement to cope with reality, we try desperately in many unrealistic ways to fulfill our needs." Doesn't this perfectly describe people without Christ? I think so. It also fits Christians who are not drawing on his available strength.

Then Dr. Glasser adds: "Therefore, essential to the fulfillment of our needs is a person, *preferably a group of peo-*

*ple* with whom we are emotionally involved from the time we are born until the time we die" (emphasis mine). He starts with "a person," whom I identify as Jesus Christ, then spreads out to a *group* of people. Now who might that be in our understanding? Wouldn't it be *the body of Christ, God's family of believers?*

On a secular level, Dr. Glasser is employing truth that you and I have learned from the Word of God. This is a tribute to his astuteness and shows us that in the field of psychology there is a swing back to a better basis of counseling, one related to truth we know from the Word of God.

But secular approaches still lack the basic ingredient—the one which makes it work. The Word of God adds that essential ingredient: "*Christ in you,* the hope of glory." He's the One who can put it all together and make it work. In counseling, you and I can offer him, the Lord of life, as the one who is available to live in every man and woman, to become to each of us the Wonderful Counselor who is the answer to *all* our problems. Christians have a decided advantage in counseling, because *we have Christ,* "in whom are hid all the treasures of wisdom and knowledge" (Col. 2:3).

## Back to Basics

It seems that what has happened over the centuries, in effect, is a great robbery. The counseling ministry has been taken away from the people of God and given to professionals —first the professional clergy, then the professional psychologist—to the detriment of the whole race. As a result, the problems faced by pastors and psychiatrists alike have become an overwhelming burden.

What God wants, I believe, is to put the ministry of counseling back on a grass-roots level in which we are bearing one another's burdens and thus strengthening one another. Counseling should be a natural part of our Christian commitment. So it's important that we Christians don't draw back and say, "I don't know enough, I'm not professionally qualified," or "Not me, I don't want to have anything to do with that. It's going to cost me, so I won't get involved." It's true that a brother whom we are counseling may for a time depend rather heavily on us, but what we need to learn is to help him move from that temporary dependence on us to a clear, forthright dependence on Jesus Christ:

He has *all* the information and *all* the wisdom.
He is on twenty-four–hour duty—which we are not.
He is always available, never out to lunch, never on vacation.
He is the one who can do the job as no one else can.
He is the counselors' Counselor.
He is the Wonderful Counselor!

With all this going for us, let's not look to psychologists to do more than they can. Without Christ, they can go only so far. Rather, let's accept the responsibility of a counseling ministry ourselves. It is clear to me that as Christians, we are not only competent to counsel but are *called* to counsel. This means that counseling is part of our *responsibility* as Christians, and, quite frankly, unless we do it, the job simply won't get done.

# CHAPTER TWO

# A Ministry of the Saints

The Apostle Paul wrote to the Roman Christians:

> We who are *strong* ought to bear with the failings of the *weak,* and not to please ourselves; let each of us please his neighbor for his good, to edify him. For Christ did not please himself; but, as it is written, "The reproaches of those who reproached thee fell on me" (Rom. 15:1–3, italics mine).

This word of instruction tells us that Christians who are strong (speaking of those who are resting in the sufficiency of a strong Lord) ought to bear the infirmities of the weak. This is another way of saying we need to "bear one another's burdens." It says that our aim in life should be for each of us "to please his neighbor for his good, to edify him." That's some statement, isn't it? What a great world it would be if we all took that word seriously!

The word "edify" here is an interesting word in the Greek text; it is literally "homebuilding." But whose home are we to be building? Ephesians tells us that Christ longs to "*settle down and be at home* in our hearts through our faith" (Eph. 3:17, freely translated). Therefore, we are to be helping one another to make each of us a comfortable place for Jesus Christ to live. This is God's "homebuilding" program.

## The Basis for Confidence

Paul, speaking to these early Roman Christians (who, you may remember, were fairly new in the Christian family), goes on to say: "I myself am satisfied about you, my brethren, that you yourselves are *full of goodness, filled with all knowledge,* and *able to instruct one another*" (Rom. 15:14, italics mine).

Note the progression of ideas here: full of goodness . . . full of knowledge . . . able to instruct.

## Full of Goodness?

The Apostle says to these relatively young believers, "I am satisfied about you, my brethren, that you yourselves are full of goodness . . ." In a recent speech, the President of the United States said he was persuaded that most politicians are good. Unfortunately, Mr. President, there is another, more authoritative voice, the Lord himself, who says politicians *aren't* good—and, of course, he includes not only politicians, but all of mankind. The Lord Jesus said, "there is none good but . . . God" (Mark 10:18, KJV). So how can we understand what Paul says to the Romans, "I am persuaded you are full of goodness"? According to our Lord, men are not *naturally* good—so where did they get this goodness? Paul is talking about the goodness God alone can give. It is part of the ninefold fruit of the Spirit mentioned in Galatians 5:22–23: "But the fruit of the Spirit is love, joy, peace, patience, kindness, *goodness,* faithfulness, gentleness, self-control; against such there is no law" (italics mine).

What does this say about Christian believers and their being qualified to counsel? It says that the counselor, first of all, has to be shaped-up himself. It says he must be in right relationship to the Lord, drawing on his goodness. Thus he will be a good person, or, to put it another way, a well-adjusted person. As long as I am part of the problem, I'll never be able to contribute much toward the solution. If I am mixed up, my counselee is probably going to be mixed up. Paul starts with, "I am persuaded that you are full of goodness." So, with us, the first step is getting our own head on straight, being sure that we have a good basis of operation in relating to our Lord—from which we are *then* able to help people.

## Filled with Knowledge

The next step in the progression is: "filled with all knowledge." This means that in order to help someone, I have to *know* something. And Paul is clearly implying that I'm not to rely on my own puny wisdom for counseling. If I did that, I would feel sorry for my counselee, for then he would be shut up to the same hangups I have. But I have knowledge that comes from God through his Word. And Paul surely has in view the information he has just imparted in this letter to the Romans. For fourteen chapters he has laid out the *basis* of human problems—and the *remedy*. He expects us to use this information.

## Able to Counsel

As we are obediently following the Lord's lead (full of goodness), and depending on his wisdom through his Word (filled with knowledge), *then* we are "able to instruct one another." Here is a significant statement relating to the subject of counseling. The key word here in the New Testament Greek is the word translated "instruct." It is a compound word made up of two parts: the Greek word for "mind" and a word meaning "to place." It is thus a word which means "to place in mind." Or to put it in more modern phraseology, we might say, "to lay to heart." It is usually translated "admonish" in the older English versions, a good translation if we understand what it means. Or, we could translate it "counsel," which would fit better into our modern concept of its meaning: you are "able to *counsel* one another."

The Greek word has two connotations, a negative and a positive. On the negative side, it has the sense of warning (and it is sometimes translated "warning" in the English text, but that brings out only half of its meaning). It also has, in the positive sense, the idea of encouragement. In practice, this means that when someone comes to us for help, we can confront him with the alternatives. First, we can show him what the end result is likely to be if he continues in the direction he's moving (if he's not obeying God's Word)—this is the warning aspect. Then, we can encourage him by clearly stating the Lord's alternative. Since he's unhappy with the situation as it stands, he may be receptive to the idea that there's a better way.

Both warning and encouragement are here: "Here is the way the Lord maps out for you. You can go that way; it's your choice. You're at the crossroads. You can go the way you're headed and ask for more of the trouble you've already experienced; you can also change your course and head in the other direction. What do you say? How about going God's way?"

That is a biblical approach to counseling—*admonishing,* or calling to mind. It is bringing the alternatives to light, presenting them, and leaving the choice with the individual. In this way we are able to help one another choose the right course of action, thus allowing the Lord to shape up our lives. Counseling is really just helping someone to live that abundant life which the Lord Jesus offers us.

But doesn't a person need to have special gifts to counsel? I don't think so, for Paul's declaration here is addressed to the *brethren,* the whole body of believers at Rome. There *are* spiritual gifts which are useful in counseling: discernment, wisdom, knowledge, exhortation, and so on; but here Paul is talking of a ministry for all Christians.

**What Do We Say?**

Where do we start? What must we learn in order to be equipped to counsel effectively? What, after all, do we have to say to people? In a key passage regarding the aim of Christian life and ministry, we read:

> To them God chose to make known how great among the Gentiles are the riches of the glory of this mystery, which is Christ in you, the hope of glory. Him we proclaim, warning every man . . . ["Warning" is that same Greek word for "counseling" or "admonishing." If we substitute *counseling,* it says something more.] . . . "counseling" every man and teaching every man in all wisdom, that we may present every man mature in Christ. For this I toil, striving with all the energy which he mightily inspires within me (Col. 1:27–29).

Here in this expression of the purpose of God in our lives (his aim is to present every man mature in Christ) this word about counseling comes up again. "Him we proclaim, 'counseling' every man . . ." Notice here that the content of our counsel is *Christ—"Him* we proclaim." So we have a clear directive as to the focus of our message. What are we to declare about him? Is it not his indwelling presence and power? We are to proclaim *Christ in you,* the hope of glory. "Glory" refers to the fulfillment of our manhood or womanhood—only possible through an indwelling Christ. God is satisfied with nothing less than our complete fulfillment, and Christ living in us is the basis on which it is designed to take place; so Paul is dealing here with essential *life in Christ.*

It is significant that we find in this text the phrase *"counseling* every man and teaching every man," as the means by which that maturing and fulfillment are to be achieved. But this counseling and teaching is to be *in all wisdom.* We do not just decide we are the great reformer of the saints—starting to buttonhole each other and saying, "I know what you need; you've got to stop operating in the flesh." No, counseling is not going around "shaping up the saints," but it is operating the way God operates—in all wisdom, drawing on his available wisdom. This means a gracious, sensitive, and firm-but-loving application of truth, not an officious, blunderbuss approach. Counseling in wisdom is obviously basic, for we see another passage connecting these two expressions: "Let the word of Christ dwell in you richly, as you teach and admonish [counsel] one another *in all wisdom,* and as you sing psalms and hymns and spiritual songs with thankfulness in your hearts to God" (Col. 3:16, italics mine). Counseling in all wisdom requires our being filled with *the word of Christ.* This is the word *from* Christ and *about* Christ. The apostle desires that *this* word may dwell in us richly. The *word* of Christ is that essential information which tells us of the person of Christ. It is not just *doctrinal* truth, but truth designed to relate us personally and directly to the living Lord who is able to fill our needs.

In both these references from Colossians notice that "admonishing and teaching" are coupled together. The use of these two words together is very significant. "Admonishing" is, as we have described it, calling to mind, laying to heart. "Teaching" is part of that process, since information must be given to form the operating basis for decisions and actions. So admonishing and teaching are a team; they go together. Our remedial and redemptive content is *Christ* and *the word of Christ;* the process is *admonishing* and *teaching.* Thus counseling becomes a matter of:

1) Learning to identify the problem from the word of Christ.
2) Knowing or finding the truth about Christ that will resolve the problem.
3) Helping our counselee discover and apply that truth.
4) Rejoicing together in the new-found liberty in Christ.

This may sound overly simplified, but quite often it's just that simple. This doesn't mean that *every* case will be decided in favor of the Lord's way, but *many* will respond to his redemptive truth. Even those who refuse the Lord's way at the time you present it may change their mind later, upon reflection, even though they may at first reject the proposed solution.

### Wisdom and Power

But all the while, we need to be checking out our resources of available wisdom and power. Remember the key principle: "Not that we are sufficient of ourselves to claim anything as coming from us; our sufficiency is from God, who has qualified us to be ministers of a new covenant . . ." (2 Cor. 3:5). The new covenant is *Christ in you,* with all that means in available resources. He is the basis of any confidence we have that we can help people find answers to life's problems. But we need wisdom, that's for sure. And we have it in Christ. In a great word about wisdom, Paul says, "He is the source of your life in Christ Jesus, whom God made our wisdom . . ." (1 Cor. 1:30). Did you catch that? Christ Jesus has been made our wisdom. He is the source of our life and our wisdom—from God. And that source ought to be wholly adequate. Remember also that in Christ "are hid all the treasures of wisdom and knowledge" (Col. 2:3).

But how are we to gain access to all this great treasure of wisdom? It's very simple really. James says, "If any of you lacks wisdom, let him ask God who gives to all men generously and without reproaching" (James 1:5). Now you have an unbeatable combination: the source and supplier of all wisdom, Jesus Christ, and the channel of access—just ask! God doesn't operate in the way we do. We say, "Hey, stupid, how come you don't know that?" God says, "I'm glad you asked, because I've just been waiting to tell you," which is enough to make us *want* to ask!

If there is anything a counselor needs besides wisdom, it's power; there is no helping people without wisdom and no changing lives without power. Have you found that out? Have you tried to change anyone lately? Sometimes you feel like trying to blast a person loose, but that won't work. Dynamite is a different kind of power, a destructive kind. But Christ, our redemptive resource, is called both "the power of God and the wisdom of God" (1 Cor. 1:24). Operating in wisdom, God's power is able to *put together* the broken pieces—not fragment and destroy, as destructive powers do.

If the wisdom and power of God aren't enough, consider: ". . . *we have the mind of Christ*" (1 Cor. 2:16). To me that is a startling statement. It doesn't mean, of course, that we always act like we have his mind, or that we always use what we have in Christ. But it means we *do* have access to the same thought processes, the same wisdom that Christ himself has. We can, through the gracious ministry of our Lord, see each situation and problem from God's perspective and apply his redemptive solution.

We need to remember, of course, that God wrote the book on the subject of man and his problems—the Bible—the book that goes with man. It is fitting that he should give us the first book on psychology, for after all, it was he who invented the human soul. He, like nobody else, knows how we operate. So if we have him as *our* counselor and his textbook in our hands, we have inside information (pun intended) and, therefore, all that we need to engage in a counseling ministry.

This premise assumes, of course, that we have a dependent, not a "cocky" attitude and that we do our homework, using every resource God has made available to us.

### Strength—But from Where?

"But wait a minute," you ask, "I'm often struggling with certain areas of weakness, and Paul says that it's the *strong* ones who should bear the iniquities of the weak. How can I counsel someone if I'm weak in the same area?" The answer is: that it has very little to do with our own strengths and weaknesses. The strength we operate from is in *Christ Jesus.*

As I understand it, when Paul speaks of "we who are strong" (Rom. 15:1), he is speaking of those who are relatively spiritually mature, who have gained a degree of equilibrium. *These* are to bear up the weaker ones. Obviously, as the Volkswagen ad says—nobody's perfect. If we wait until we have arrived at perfection, we will never start. So, the word "strong" here is a relative term and is really referring us back to the strength that is in Christ, the power that comes from him.

Haven't you discovered that God will often bring you together with someone who is having the same struggle in which you have recently experienced his victory? It is not so that *you* can strengthen that friend, but so you can *share* the reality of God's strength in your common weakness. If we are rightly related to him, we are drawing on his strength; it isn't ours, it is a borrowed strength. You are weak, I am weak, we're all weak, since we all share the same frail humanity. That's one of the features which makes us suited to counsel. If we are up on a pedestal of spiritual superiority, shooting our thunderbolts of judgmental censure down on the poor peons below, then we are already out of the business. It is the recognition of the common humanity we share which makes us ready and able to counsel.

One of the first things necessary in counseling is to identify with the problem of the person before us. We must be able to say, "I've been there, too, but I have discovered an answer to my frailty in that particular area of failure, and I would like to share that answer with you." There is an old saying which says, "A Christian is just one beggar telling another beggar where he found bread." That's the idea; we don't preach ourselves, but Jesus as Lord, and thereby we offer the liberty that his Lordship brings—to us and to any who will let him be Lord.

Because we do identify with others in their weakness, there is no more demanding and draining ministry than counseling. This is partly because the Lord will get to *you*, the counselor, in the process (and show you where you are not making it). The counselor is always part of the target area in the Lord's character-building program, and that always takes an emotional toll. But in addition to that, we hurt with those who are hurting. It's part of the process.

All of this does not imply that we will always see the answers and that referrals are not sometimes indicated and necessary. There should be the recognition that our weaknesses sometimes limit our insight into truth and that we may find an area where we cannot help but someone else can. Making referrals and using other resource people is thus both valid and sensible. Conferring with other (perhaps more mature and more experienced) counselors is wise procedure, if for no other reason than to confirm the validity of one's own analysis and approach to the problem.

# CHAPTER THREE

## Preview of the Process

Perhaps you have sensed the possibility that you may have already been involved in a sort of counseling ministry without being aware of it. You probably don't think of yourself as a *counselor,* and yet there may have been times in your life as a Christian when someone has talked about his problems or struggles with you, and you perhaps thought of a verse of Scripture that could throw some light on the situation. Or maybe you simply listened and empathized with him, feeling helpless but wanting to help. Perhaps all you could do was to encourage the person in his faith, reassuring him that God is to be trusted. If you've been in this sort of situation, you have the idea. The desire to counsel is there, within you, but you may not know how to go about it. Before we go any farther, I'd like to whet your appetite with a simple outline of the process of effective counseling.

First, let's observe that there are at least two types of counseling we may encounter as Christians:

1) The informal kind, growing out of an established, ongoing relationship.

2) The more formalized situation where we are counseling someone whom we may not know at all but who has come to us for help.

Many of this second type grow out of our teaching or leadership ministries, such as teaching a Bible class or acting as discussion leader or advisor to any of the various groups in the church. Let's consider this more formal demand first, since much of what we do in this kind of situation will apply to the other, more informal kind as well.

## A Simple Procedure

We need to approach a counseling ministry with some basic principles in mind. Here are my suggestions:

1) Listen—with compassion. Help them be at ease. Identify with them.

2) Ask God for wisdom to discern the *real* problem.

3) Highlight the net results of the alternative courses of action on a factual, non-judgmental basis.

4) Apply Christ's "Formula for Freedom" (John 8:31–32).

5) Help them discover the Lord's alternative to failure.

6) Don't tell them what to do; leave the decision squarely on them as to which way they choose.

7) Remind them they will live with the results.

8) Pray *with* them and *for* them.

## First–Listen!

The counselor's first assignment is to be a good listener. This means that the first twenty to forty minutes of an interview will usually be listening—with an occasional leading question or a gentle nudge to get them back on the main track. We must consider our counselee the most important person in our program for the time we are together. No preoccupation factors are permissible! How do *you* like pouring your heart out to someone who isn't paying attention?

## With Compassion

If you are mentally or emotionally "out to lunch," you are absolutely no good to your counselee! Compassion is "feeling

with," and unless they sense our empathy, they might as well talk to a brick wall. That doesn't mean we are to say, "Oh, you poor thing! You've really been wronged." Sympathy of this kind is probably the last thing they need. They just need to know we care.

## Help Them Be at Ease

It's very hard to unload our innermost feelings and problems to *anyone,* especially to one we may have never seen before. Our counselee doesn't know if this character in front of him is going to scold him, scathe him, or scald him. He usually has a well-developed guilt syndrome—so he fears the worst. What he really *hopes* for is to be loved and understood, at least—maybe even helped!

So, when our counselee first enters the scene, we should seek a way to help him relax. Usually he will say, "I don't know where to start." So we can take the pressure off by saying something like, "Well then, why don't you let me start? I'd like to tell you about me: I'm just here to help; I don't have any magical powers; I'm no psychologist; I'm just God's man (or God's woman); and if I can, I want to help you find out what he can do for you. And I've found out he can do plenty! He's the One to whom I look for help. Now, why don't you start by trying to state the problem, as you see it, in one sentence?"

Or perhaps you see them sitting on the edge of their chair and say, "You look all tensed up. Won't you sit back and relax?" Or you might offer them a cup of coffee, or compliment them on their clothes, or hair style, or whatever good feature you observe.

## Identify with Them

Somehow, and as early as possible in the interview, you must let them know you share the same frail, fallible humanity. This is not hard if you look for an opportunity, because you *do* share a common, fractured human nature. Let them know it!

### Ask God for Wisdom

As you listen—pray. For apart from your discernment of their *real* problem (which *may* or *may not* be the one they state) there is no way you can help. We don't want to end up just treating symptoms; we'd like to see God use us to cure the disease! Our genuine dependence on the Wonderful Counselor at this point is crucial.

### Highlight Results of Alternative Courses

An objective appraisal of the results of their present course and a projected look at the changes the Lord's way would make can comprise a rather attractive package. This assumes you can present this on a totally redemptive, non-condemning basis. Counselees don't need or want a scolding. But they will usually welcome a constructive proposal which holds the promise of better days ahead.

### Christ's Formula for Freedom

How simply and concisely our Lord put it: "If you continue in my word, you are truly my disciples, and you will know the truth, and the truth will make you free" (John 8:31–32). In 20th-century American language the Lord Jesus is giving us four simple points:

1) "Just keep doing what I'm telling you."

2) "Then you'll be learning what it's all about" (a disciple is a "learner").

3) "You will know the truth." (You won't be just drifting in a swamp of opinion, but you'll be achored to reality.)

4) "The truth will set you free."

And freedom is what everybody's looking for! The word in our day is "liberation": women's liberation, gay liberation —it's even a favorite word of the communists! But, to alter the lyrics of an old Negro spiritual, "Everyone who's talking 'bout liberation ain't liberated." A telling example of this fact is the inscription we see in marble on many college and university campuses: "YOU SHALL KNOW THE TRUTH AND THE TRUTH SHALL SET YOU FREE."

In that context, the idea is apparently that education is liberation. But this word about liberation is true only if we keep it in the biblical context. It is only our response to the Liberator himself, the Lord Jesus, that results in *true* liberation. Education literally means "to lead out." If our education relates to learning how Christ can "lead us out" of our problems and hurts, then education *can* result in liberation. This is the kind of education and liberation we need to employ as Christian counselors. Incidentally, freedom is *not* just "doing as I please" but rather, *being what God designed me to be*—an important distinction to make in our counseling.

### Help Them Discover

There's an old rule of pedagogy that says, "Don't ever tell your students what they can discover for themselves." This is a good approach to counseling, as well. But help them discover what?

### The Lord's Alternative to Failure

What counselees need is to find the way the Lord has made to handle their present dilemma. Incidentally, he always has a way; he is never stumped on a problem. That's nice to know.

Usually the ones seeking help are already sick of the way they've been handling things. So, quite often, their hearts are conditioned to respond if we can give them a reasonable alternative to their "status quo." (Status quo, in case you've forgotten, is Latin for "the mess we're in.")

### Don't Tell Them What to Do

Giving advice is a trap counselors fall into rather easily. I have learned, the hard way, to avoid this temptation. Usually, when someone asks for my advice, I tell them, "It will be worth every penny you'll pay for it—zero."

But what do we mean by "giving advice"? It's like this. Someone tells you their situation and asks, "What do you think I ought to do?" This question is invalid on two counts: It is shifting the responsibility for decision off them and onto you; it ignores the right of Christ to exercise his Lordship in their life. And invariably, when we mistakenly tell people what we think they should do, it boomerangs. They come back later and tell us, "I did what you advised and it didn't work!" Then what do we say?

So, *we don't give advice.*

### Leave the Decision Squarely on Them

Jesus is Lord, and our counselees should be taught to ask *him* what to do. We must be careful not to usurp our Lord's prerogative to be what he designs to be to every Christian—our *Lord* Jesus Christ. As counselors, we *can* help them see what he has said in his Word, in specific commands, or promises, or in terms of broad operating principles. This is our place of ministry.

### Remind Them They Will Live with Their Choice

If there is resistance to God's Word and will, we need to help people see the obvious fact: They are stuck with the status quo. If there is compliance, we have the joy of sharing in their new-found liberty and pointing out the bright prospect God has for them through his redemptive grace. Thus, we can encourage and help them to keep on trusting the Lord.

**Pray with Them and for Them**

This is many times the most profitable time we have with them. I've found it very heartening to have another Christian bear us up before the Lord in prayer. It does two things: It brings the Lord directly into the action on a very realistic basis; it places their dependence (and ours) squarely on the Lord's ability to handle the situation. But when you pray, make it a genuine placing of the real issues squarely before the Lord with no fancy phrases—just straight talk.

So much for our approach to a formal counseling interview. But these same principles apply to the informal counseling opportunities; the basic difference in procedure is the time element. With the "friendship" kind of situation we have the luxury of waiting for opportunities to speak, and moving at a more leisurely pace.

**Now–The Hard Part**

A Christian counselor *must be* a man or woman of the Word of God. We must know specific truth to apply or we cannot prescribe in accord with Christ's "Formula for Freedom." Generalities won't do; we soon find that out. If we splash some neat little Christian cliché on them like, "Just pray about it" or "Just turn it over to the Lord," we are offering them only frustration and defeat. So we must do our homework, being lifetime students of God's Word. Counseling is a one-on-one teaching ministry of *applying the truth to life*—so it demands a clear knowledge of the Word of God and how it applies to life's problems. It also demands *speaking the truth in love.* We cannot let our desire to be popular keep us from "leveling" with them about their problem. Sometimes the truth hurts, but it also *heals.* And if we believe our Lord in John 8:31–32, it's *the only way to real freedom.* We must be willing to risk friendship and popularity, if necessary, to help them. Otherwise we're not acting in love.

On the other hand, we can't just plaster Scripture verses on them like biblical Band-Aids in calloused unconcern, without compassion.

In addition to what we have reviewed on *counseling procedures* and *knowledge of the truth,* we need *a basic philosophy* from which to operate. I'd like to propose that our biblical approach to counseling be something like this:

> We believe that: ALL HUMAN PROBLEMS AND HURTS ARE SOMEHOW A CONSEQUENCE OF SIN. SO WE MUST APPROACH A COUNSELING MINISTRY WITH SOME UNDERSTANDING OF SIN AND ITS CONSEQUENCES—THEN APPLY THE REDEMPTIVE TRUTH OF GOD TO THE PROBLEM.

The beginning of that understanding necessary for a fruitful counseling ministry is only possible if we seek to understand the problem—and the problem is sin. So we need to grasp the psychology of sin, or *how sin affects our souls.* I think you'll be amazed at the change in your own understanding and attitude toward sin (and God) as you follow the action of the next chapters. Unless, you're afraid to look!

CHAPTER FOUR

# In the Beginning

Sin is a vastly misunderstood subject. If we should ask a hundred people at random what sin is and what it does, we would get a hodge-podge of answers. Most of the answers would probably revolve around the idea that sin describes everything I like to do, and everything I like to do turns out to be illegal, immoral, or fattening. Many have the idea God is "that old killjoy" who makes me feel guilty any time I'm having fun. Nothing could be further from the truth. God *loves* us and *hates* sin because it hurts us.

**Who Started It?**

To gain initial perspective on the problems sin has imposed on the race, we need to see how it all began and where it led. Wouldn't it be interesting to hear from the original problem pair on the subject? Their explanation of the matter might be something like this:

I AM EVE . . .

(A short, short story with a long ending.)

"I am Eve. And I'd like to explain what happened . . .

"We were really very happy, Adam and I. He was a wonderful man—my man, with a grace and glow about him that called forth the love and devotion of my heart. And Eden was something else! Everything anyone could want, we thought, including God himself, who filled our lives with his presence and gave us everything we needed to make life full and happy.

"But then something happened . . .

"One of God's most beautiful creatures (I found later it was a disguise; he is really very ugly) came to me with a suggestion. He said, 'Is it true that God told you not to eat from every tree in the garden?'

"You know, until he brought it up I never thought much about it, but now I saw that God was really holding out on us! There was this *one* tree in the middle of the garden from which God had said we were not to eat.

"So I replied, 'You're right, there's that one tree whose fruit God told us not to eat, or even to touch. He said we would die if we ate it.'

" '*But you won't die,*' he said. 'God knows when you eat it you'll learn something and you'll be like God.'

"Now that made sense. I'd already noticed that the fruit looked good to eat. It was beautiful to see. I could almost taste it. Such luscious beauty was bound to taste great. And besides, didn't God want us to discover and explore the garden? After all, it was our domain!

"So I tasted it! I even shared it with my husband; I shared everything with him because God had made us one.

"But then I had some second thoughts because suddenly I felt insecure and naked. And Adam had somehow faded. He had lost that glow of manhood I loved so much.

"So we went and hid—and I learned to sew fig leaves.

"We learned something all right—at least the shining beast spoke the truth about that. But what we learned we could have done without! That beautiful, deceitful creature did us no favor. Before, we were perfectly at ease with each other and with God. We had nothing to feel ashamed about, no insecurity. Now we were haunted with that vague uneasiness we both hate.

"But why should we be uncomfortable before God? He's the one who loved us and made the garden so great for us to live in!

"Want to know how I got out of line?

"Well, I hate to admit it, but I'm an emotional creature, and I just indulged in a bit of emotional rationalization. I knew God had said, 'Don't eat of that fruit,' but I let my own senses convince me that I knew better than God, and of course, I had some help from that lying, insinuating beast!

"Don't get me wrong, there's nothing wrong with being emotional. After all, God made me that way. But to make judgments *against* what God says is more than a simple emotional hangup—it's spiritual suicide.

"And you know what? I never once checked with Adam. I just assumed he would do what I wanted and caught him in the same web of deceit.

"What have I learned?

"Well, first, God wasn't fooling—we died! He means what he says and has the sovereign right to make it stick. And I guess, since he made us, he has a right to make the rules.

"Oh, in case you wondered, we didn't die physically that day, but we sure found out we were uncomfortable about God, both emotionally and spiritually. We sensed our separation from him. We died that way. We began to feel out of step, frustrated, and exposed. More than that, we began to inherit aches and pains in bodies that were now exposed to all sorts of ills. We knew evil all right—in bodies that began to die, and in souls and spirits that *were* dead, cut off from the life of God!

"What else did I learn? We became the slaves of the one we obeyed—that lying beast! And we were sent out of that perfect place, our home, to taste the futility of messed-up lives in a mixed-up world.

"I was fooled. And what a fool I was!"

I AM ADAM . . .

"I am Adam, and I'd like to add a word here.

"It wasn't really Eve's fault. Eve was fooled, but I wasn't. I just stood there and let her get taken. Why did I do it? I was just plain willful! God had explained about the tree, but I just flat-out rebelled! And talk about a fool—I knew the score and *still* fell for that lying insinuation, because I *wanted* to.

"It wasn't enough to have 'all this and heaven, too.' I had to defy authority. So I'm the one to blame for the fix we're in. You can lay it on me for all the blood, sweat, and tears. I messed it up. I introduced all the evil—the hatred and inequity and pollution—the nature of sin in the race. Before, we only knew good and knew nothing of evil. Now we've got the whole bag, and who needs it?

"By the way, in case you think it's big of me to admit it; it wasn't always that way. When God first asked me about it, I blamed him! I said, 'This woman *you gave me,* gave me the fruit.' And Eve said, 'The beast beguiled me.' This was the original buck-passing act.

"I'm telling you this so you can be more of a man than I was. At least, don't blame your wife. *And don't blame God!*

"Can you imagine? God came looking for me! I clearly remember him saying, 'Where are you, Adam?'

"Not that he didn't know where I was, but he wanted *me* to find out where I was—with him.

"Know what I found?

*"He still loved me!"*

**But God, Who Is Great in Mercy**

God showed his love to Adam and Eve, even while he was declaring what the consequences of their sin would be. (Sin *always* has consequences, as we will see in some detail in the next chapter.) God gave them hope, as they cowered ashamedly before him, telling them of the "seed of the woman," who would bruise the serpent's head. He was referring to the coming Savior who would defeat the adversary, Satan.

When God had finished questioning the guilty pair (not accusing them), he made garments for them out of skins to replace their self-made coverings. The skin clothing provided by God pictures the righteousness God supplies through the shedding of blood, given to take the place of man's self-righteous attempts at cover-up.

## The Long Ending

The rest of the story is the subject of the whole biblical record and is summarized in passages like this one from Romans 5:

> This, then, is what has happened. Sin made its entry into the world through one man, and through sin, death. The entail of sin and death passed on to the whole human race, and no one could break it for no one was himself free from sin. . . .
>
> Adam, the first man, corresponds in some degree to the man who was to come. But the gift of God through Christ is a very different matter from the "account rendered" through the sin of Adam. For while as a result of one man's sin death by natural consequence became the common lot of men, it was by the generosity of God, the free giving of the grace of the one man Jesus Christ, that the love of God overflowed for the benefit of all men. . . .
>
> For if one man's offense meant that men should be slaves to death all their lives, it is a far greater thing that through another man, Jesus Christ, men by their acceptance of his more than sufficient grace and righteousness should live all their lives like kings!
>
> We see, then, that as one act of sin exposed the whole race of men to God's judgment and condemnation, so one act of perfect righteousness presents all men freely acquitted in the sight of God. (Commentary on man's fall from Romans 5:12–19 by the Apostle Paul, Phillips New Testament.)

This description of the antidote to sin's problems provided in Jesus Christ, when added to the verses just before these in Romans 5, tells the wonderful story of God's remedy for sin's devastation in the redemptive grace of the Lord Jesus:

> Therefore, since we are justified by faith, we have peace with God through our Lord Jesus Christ. Through him we have obtained access to this grace in which we stand, and we rejoice in our hope of sharing the glory of God.
>
> While we were yet helpless, at the right time Christ died for the ungodly. Why, one will hardly die for a righteous man—though perhaps for a good man one will dare even to die. But God shows his love for us in that while we were yet sinners Christ died for us. Since, therefore, we are now justified by his blood, much more shall we be saved by him from the wrath of God. For if while we were enemies we were reconciled to God by the death of his Son, much more, now that we are reconciled, shall we be saved by his life (Romans 5:1–2, 6–10).

We are *reconciled* (restored to harmony again) to God by Christ's *death*—and *saved* (rescued from present and future futility) by his *resurrection life!* That's what God has done about sin! We are *restored* in our relationship to God as we receive Christ and the value of his death and *rehabilitated* as we keep drawing by faith on his indwelling life! This is a program secular counselors cannot offer, for they neither understand it nor believe it. Only a Christian counselor can offer these redemptive values to a world in trouble.

It is possible to list the redemptive answer to every human problem, and the verses of Scripture which explain it, if we will just do our homework and seek to know the Word of God. This is the Christian counselor's task. In order to make a beginning on what is really a lifetime pursuit, we endeavored to do this in regard to some of the basic problems we frequently encounter, like fear, guilt, anxiety, and so on. Several listings, with applicable Scriptures, were prepared by one of our adult elective classes on counseling and are included in the Appendix.*

---

* See Appendix A, "Spiritual Principles of Counseling," and Appendix B, "Sins and Solutions," two excellent analyses of some of the counseling problems we encounter, with their biblical solutions, by Paul Leavenworth and Charlotte Mersereau, two keen students in one of our counselor training classes.

CHAPTER FIVE

# The Psychology of Sin

Understanding the concept of sin is basic to our understanding of ourselves, our insight into the problems that surround us in the world today, and most important of all, our knowledge of God. Through such understanding we are enabled to grasp the reason behind man's basic insecurity with its accompaniment on one hand of overwhelming feelings of inferiority or, on the other hand, the bluff and bluster of man's colossal conceit—the cover-up for insecurity.

As we understand sin, we also begin to understand man's insatiable quest for knowledge, originally God-given, which has become a misguided attempt on man's part to prove his own fancied self-sufficiency. "You will be as God" was the promise, the lying insinuation of Satan. Yet we are not independently self-sufficient as God is. God is still waiting patiently in the wings, still *sovereign,* still *the author of life,* still *the great supplier* of all our needs, still *longing* for us to come to our senses and *acknowledge* our utter dependence on him. In spite of all attempts to bolster our ego through the accumulation of knowledge, we still seem to know inherently that we have made a moral overdraft on our account, with insufficient funds to cover the debt—and that no amount of mere knowledge or intellect will supply the deficit. Man is ever learning and yet never coming to the knowledge of the truth as it is in Jesus. We know so much but understand so little. Yet we find it so hard to admit our spiritual poverty.

Now, for additional perspective about sin, let's examine the meaning of the words for sin in biblical Greek and Hebrew. In this way we can regain some of the original sense God intends for us to understand in his Word about sin, the problems it creates, and God's means for solving those problems.*

## Old Testament Concepts

First let's consider the Old Testament words referring to sin. One of the Hebrew words for sin that is most frequently used is *chatáh,* which means "to miss the right point" and describes those who have lost their way—who even with the best of intentions are still off the track. Another word, *shaláh,* means "to err," that is, doing that which is not done—that which is unacceptable conduct. Two other words have the sense "to rebel"—the Hebrew *pasha* and *marad.*

Right away we can see that the Old Testament idea of sin recognizes a *standard of acceptable behavior* (specified by God) from which men depart. It's an easy step from there to an attitude of rebellion which brings with it a sense of guilt. Feelings of guilt are caused by departure from God's norm, attended by a sense of opposition to God, who has authority to call us to account.

In addition there is also the idea of acting in some degree of ignorance, implying a clouded mind incapable of assessing the consequences of unacceptable actions. Beyond this, the Hebrew concept of sin also includes the idea of *uncleanness:* Sin makes men polluted and unfit for fellowship with God, who is spotlessly holy.

So in the Old Testament concept of sin we have these ideas:

- Sin is *missing the right point.*
- Sin is *unacceptable conduct.*

* Much helpful material for this chapter has been gleaned from *Theological Dictionary of the New Testament,* ed. G. Kittel and G. Friedrich, 8 vols. (Grand Rapids, Mich.: Eerdmans, 1964-72).

- Sin is *rebellion against authority.*
- Sin contains an element of *ignorance.*
- Sin *makes unclean.*

The net result for man is an uneasy sense of guilt and frustration—a sense of alienation from God and fear of facing him in life or in death. It's easy to see that these factors describe the common state of mankind, reflected by the unrest of his heart in the presence of God and the sense of frustration and futility which is our common lot.

It is not much of a step from this sense of futility to the current phenomenon of flagrant deviation from required norms and the ultimate repudiation of *every* norm—the swamp of moral relativism in which much of the world lives today. Our understanding of sin should give us insight into the current trends of thought and life if we are to supply genuine answers to the real needs of real people.

## The Rock of Truth

In the midst of the confusion brought about by relativism, the revealed truth of the Bible tells of a God who sovereignly reigns, and against whose authority man only breaks *himself.* It is no wonder, then, that the Bible makes a valiant effort to show man the folly of *missing the right point,* whether in rebellion or in ignorance. No wonder it reveals the antidote to sin and guilt with pleading power and shows us how to be free from that feeling of dread which makes us want to flee from the greatness of God and our ultimate accountability to him.

But the sense of sin and guilt also has its useful side. Guilt is to the soul of man much like pain is to the body. It can be used by God to show us that we have violated not just human standards of conduct, the mores of man's making, but rather we have violated *God's* norms. The relative weight of sins in man's view is not the question–instead, we are "missing out" through life's frustrations because we have *missed the point of God's plan.* The true sense of sin and *real* guilt are God-given to lead us back to a right relationship with him. Thus the question is not *how* we missed the point, whether guilt is incurred through a mistake or in conscious rebellion. The result is still the same: guilty feelings and a sense of uncleanness, which must somehow be removed. In sinning there is always an element either of bad judgment or of outright rebellion which must be dealt with by God.

For example, at the beginning of the race, Eve was deceived and sinned while Adam sinned willfully: ". . . and Adam was not deceived, but the woman was deceived and became a transgressor" (1 Tim. 2:14). Note that Eve is called a *transgressor* even though she was deceived. To set aside guilt, from whatever cause, requires the same atoning sacrifice even though outright rebellion may make us more culpable, for *guilt is the debt incurred by acts of sin* and somehow the debt must be paid off.

## The Truth about Consequences

In the Scriptures the original pair is a picture preview of us all. We can all be trusted to act and react the same way they did. The *consequences of sin* are being lived out in our own experience in the same way as in the experience of the original pair. Looking from their experience to our own, we can discover these consequences:

- An attempt to "cover up."
- A tendency to shift any blame off ourselves.
- A sense of guilt and unacceptability.
- A desire to escape the consequences of our wrong acts.
- A drive for knowledge to bolster our ego.
- Attempts to pit our vaunted intellect against the knowledge of God.
- Operating from our own mind set and/or sensual drives.

- Minds beset with the cold power of doubt, with its attendant insecurity.
- Rejecting of any idea of uncritical obedience to revealed truth about God.
- Flaunting of God's sovereign authority.
- Being stuck with our own stupidity.
- Falling heir to all the frustration and futility of life without God, which is in reality the "walking death" inherited from Adam.
- Living in a world of illusion.

  Finding all the wrong answers to the right questions because we fail to see that, ". . . the Lord gives wisdom; from his mouth come knowledge and understanding" (Prov. 2:6), and "The fear of the Lord is the beginning of wisdom, and the knowledge of the Holy One is insight" (Prov. 9:10).
- By believing the lie, we become slaves of the one we obey—dupes subject to Satanic power and influence.
- Finally, we become God's critics.

Writing about the Genesis account of the entrance of sin into the race, Gottfried Tuell declares:

> The narrator [of Genesis] consciously emphasizes the demonic nature of the thought which derives from doubt, which strives fanatically for knowledge and which for the sake of it tears down everything that would hamper it. He gives us to understand that a kind of alien power comes over the man who sins, which he must obey against his better judgment because it convinces him by its assured manner and its correspondence with his own feeling.
>
> Because man seeks to be wise irrespective of God's authority, because he seeks to penetrate behind the thoughts of God and to anticipate them, because he not only wills to do this but is able to do so within certain limits, a sphere of mistrust is opened up in which it is possible and tempting for man to renounce the attitude appropriate to him as a creature, to regard the creator with criticism and *to think and act as himself God,* unhampered, and responsible only to himself.*

---

* In *Theological Dictionary of the New Testament,* 8 vols., ed. G. Kittel and G. Friedrich (Grand Rapids, Mich.: Eerdmans, 1964-72). Used by permission.

## Tracking Down the Greek

Our understanding of the psychology of sin can be further enhanced by examining the unfolding pattern in the history of Greek thought, leading up to the ultimate usage of the Greek words for sin in the New Testament. The most commonly-used word for sin in the Greek New Testament is *hamartiá* and its related forms, used some 217 times. The use of this one word, traced through the golden age of the Greek philosophers, is like a floodlight on the patterns of worldly thought, not only in ancient Greece but in today's thinking as well.

Aristotle defines *hamartiá* as, "A missing of virtue, the desired goal, whether out of weakness, accident or defective knowledge." His definition involved no concept of *guilt*. Not until this word was used in the Septuagint version of the Old Testament was it invested with the idea of being an *offense* against God. In the Septuagint, the Greek translation of the Hebrew Scriptures, the revelation of God was added to man's wisdom as expressed through the Greek philosophers.

The biblical view of sin is not found in classical Greek, for in Greek thought there was no sense of man expressing enmity against God in his refusal to yield to God's authority and do his will. *Hamartiá,* in its classical Greek usage, covers everything from crime to harmless faults. It includes:

- Artistic and intellectual defects.
- Technical and hygienic failures.
- Errors of judgment on the part of legislators.
- Political blunders.
- And finally, ethical failures mistakenly performed in good faith, but done through non-culpable ignorance.

In Aristotle's definition, virtue was not an absolute, but it was the mean between two extremes. Any deviation from that mean, to either extreme, was considered *hamartiá.*

*Hamartiá,* then, was *doing that which is not intellectually or technically correct* in accordance with the Greek mores. There were no moral implications connected with *hamartiá,* since a man deviating from the mean was simply acting out of the inescapable ignorance to which he was bound. No *real* sense of guilt was inferred. In this view all guilt was derived from ignorance, but since ignorance is a limitation of human existence imposed by fate, man deserves no blame.

## The Tragedy of Greek Tragedy

The meaning of the Greek tragedy is anchored in this concept: Human guilt follows from the limitation of human knowledge—not as personal, moral guilt, but as guilt given with existence itself. Man acts in ignorance, with unforeseeable consequences for which he is not responsible. All he can do is accept the consequences of his ignorant error. The result: *tragedy, with no remedy.*

Socrates based his work of instruction on the principle that ignorance is the root of all evil. It follows that for the Greek philosopher *right understanding will lead to right action;* the man who really understands and knows, acts rightly. And, of course, behind this assumption stands the belief that man is basically good.

In all this we see the background of more modern thought: The view that wrong actions of men stem from ignorance which can be removed by education, thus avoiding any thought of personal responsibility or guilt. Solon, another Greek philosopher, put it this way: "According to the immanent laws of developing reality, according to the law of time, the bad withers and the good flourishes and establishes itself." Or, putting it all together: It's inevitable that things will get better and better, education will produce right behavior, and man (being basically good) only needs to learn and he will behave.

The factor obviously lacking in this philosophy, from the

Christian view, is the will of fallen man by which he expresses his defiance of God and His Word.

## Sin in the New Testament

*Hamartiá* achieves a moral and spiritual meaning in the New Testament by a dual process in which (1) words first employed about the natural and physical realm of life are eventually transferred into usage encompassing the moral and spiritual realm, and (2) God takes these words and invests them with still deeper meaning as they are employed by him in the biblical revelation of truth.

We can discover some of this added meaning by examining both the derivation and development of the words themselves and then by viewing their usage in the context of the New Testament. Before we do this, though, we want first to look at the etymology of *hamartiá*. In Trench's *Synonyms of the New Testament,* we discover that the derivation of this word is a bit obscure and uncertain, yet there are certain intriguing possibilities. The first of these is the conjecture that *hamartiá* may derive from *márptō,* "to grasp." If *márptō* is coupled with the letter *alpha,* the sense is negated, and we have *hamarptiá,* or "a failing to grasp." Another possibility is that it may stem from *méros,* meaning "part" or "share," from which a negative verb was formed meaning "to be without one's share, to miss out."

While these possible derivations are interesting, the more certain meaning is derived from an observation of the use and scope of the word in Greek writings, especially in the New Testament. Trench summarizes his own understanding of *hamartiá* by the statement: "Only this much is plain, that when sin is contemplated as *hamartiá* it is regarded as a *failing and missing the true end and scope of our lives, which is God.*" Thus *hamartiá* signifies "missing the mark," being the exact opposite of the Greek word for "hitting the mark, to attain, to achieve." Trench adds that in secular Greek this word is used of a poet who selects a subject which is impossible to treat poetically or who seeks to attain results which lie beyond the limits of his art (Aristotle, Poët, 8 and 25).

It appears obvious that if sin truly involves missing the point of our life and existence, then an understanding of sin should drastically alter our whole approach to life, particularly our attitude toward God, for no one really wants to *miss out* on anything good, *especially when it involves missing the whole point of one's life and reason for being*.

As we look now at New Testament usage, with this definitive research data in our minds, the light of clearer understanding should break through regarding the deep significance of "sin" as revealed in God's Word. The starting point in this part of our investigation is Romans 3:23: ". . . since all have sinned [*hamartánein*] and fall short of the glory of God." The addition of the words, "fall short of the glory of God," is helpful confirmation of the sense of "missing the mark" implicit in *hamartiá*. Add to this our Lord's words in John 8:24: ". . . for you will die in your sins [*hamartiá*] unless you believe that I am he." Here we have the fatal consequences of sin declared and the remedy offered—in the Son sent from the Father to redeem man.

To summarize the far-reaching effects of sin implied or pointed out in the uses of *hamartiá* in the New Testament the following charts may be helpful.

In this charted form, we have summarized over sixty of the more than 200 occurrences of *hamartiá* in the New Testament. It's remarkable to see what a clear overview it gives us to list the occurrences of this word under these headings. If you were to review the remaining references to *hamartiá*, using a guide such as *Englishman's Greek Concordance*, you would undoubtedly learn even more about God's view of sin and its effects in our lives.

| CHART I | THE EFFECTS OF SIN |
|---|---|
| (1) WHAT SIN IS | Not acting in faith (Rom. 14:23).<br>The product of desire (Jas. 1:15).<br>Not doing what we know we should (Jas. 4:17).<br>Transgression (1 Jn. 3:4).<br>Lawlessness (1 Jn. 3:4).<br>All unrighteousness is sin (1 Jn. 5:17). |
| (2) WHAT SIN DOES | Brings death (Rom. 6:16, 23; 7:5, 11).<br>Enslaves us (Rom. 6:17, 20; Jn. 8:34).<br>Deceives us (Rom. 7:11; Heb. 3:13).<br>Gives certain pleasures (Heb. 11:25).<br>Surrounds us (Heb. 12:1).<br>Can be against our own body (1 Cor. 6:18).<br>Can be against our own brothers (1 Cor. 8:12).<br>Can be fatal (1 Jn. 5:16; Heb. 10:26). |
| (3) WHO SIN TOUCHES | *All* under sin (Rom. 3:9; Gal. 3:22).<br>Both Jew and Gentile (Rom. 2:12).<br>*All* have sinned (Rom. 3:23). |

| CHART II | GOD'S REMEDY FOR SIN—CHRIST IN THE LIFE |
|---|---|
| (1) HOW CHRIST DEALT WITH SIN | Where sin abounded, grace all the more (Rom. 5:20).<br>Christ died for our sins (1 Cor. 15:3).<br>God made him (Christ) to be sin for us (2 Cor. 5:21).<br>In Christ we have redemption, the forgiveness of sins (Col. 1:14).<br>He, by himself, purged our sins (Heb. 1:3).<br>He put away sin by the sacrifice of himself (Heb. 9:26).<br>He bore our sins in his own body (1 Pet. 2:24).<br>His blood keeps on cleansing us from sin (1 Jn. 1:7).<br>If we confess our sins, he forgives (1 Jn. 1:9).<br>He is the propitiation for our sins (1 Jn. 2:2).<br>He was manifested to take away our sins (1 Jn. 3:5).<br>He loosed us from our sins (Rev. 1:5).<br>BUT ALSO<br>Christ's coming exposed sin (Jn. 15:22, 24). |

| | THE CHRISTIAN AND SIN | THE NON-CHRISTIAN AND SIN |
|---|---|---|
| (2) THE DIFFERENCE CHRIST MAKES | Sin not charged (Rom. 4:8).<br>Dead to sin (Rom. 6:2, 7, 11; 1 Pet. 2:24).<br>Not sin's slave (Rom. 6:6, 12, 14, 17).<br>Free from sin (Rom. 6:22; 8:2).<br>Yet sin still a problem (Rom. 7:14, 17, 20).<br>We still sin (1 Jn. 1:8–10).<br>But we don't *practice* sin (1 Jn. 3:9).<br>It's not for us (1 Jn. 2:1).<br>Abiding in Christ keeps us from sinning (1 Jn. 3:6). | Sin reigns (Rom. 5:21).<br>Dead in sins (Eph. 2:1).<br>Are of the devil (1 Jn. 3:8).<br>Are dying in sins (Jn. 8:24). |

## The Greeks Had a Word for It

*Hamartiá,* however, is not the only word used for sin in the New Testament. Several other words each give a different dimension to the concept of sin. Here are some of them:

*Asébeia:* "Godlessness"—living and acting as though God didn't exist, or if he does, we owe him nothing. Ruling God out, refusing to give to God the thanks and worship due him. Romans 1:18 illustrates: "For the wrath of God is revealed from heaven against all ungodliness [*asébeia*] and wickedness of men who . . . suppress the truth."

*Parakóē:* "Disobedience" resulting from a refusal to listen—being inattentive to what God has to say. Romans 5:19 illustrates: "For as by one man's disobedience [*parakóē*] many were made sinners, so by one man's obedience many will be made righteous." (Also compare Heb. 2:1–3.)

*Paráptoma:* "A blunder," or deviation from the right, failure to act in accord with the standard. Galatians 6:1 illustrates: "Brethren, if a man is overtaken in any trespass [*paráptoma*], you who are spiritual should restore him in a spirit of gentleness."

*Parábasis:* "Transgression," conscious crossing of a divinely appointed boundary, trespassing into areas clearly proscribed. Romans 2:23 illustrates: "You who boast in the law, do you dishonor God by breaking [*parábasis*] the law?"

*Anomía:* "Lawlessness," deliberate disregard of God's laws by acting contrary to them in a spirit of rebellion. 1 John 3:4 illustrates: "Every one who commits sin is guilty of lawlessness [*anomía*]; sin is lawlessness" (i.e. *hamartía* is *anomía*).

*Hḗttēma:* "Defeat," failure to appropriate available resources, thereby accepting failure as inevitable. 1 Corinthians 6:7 illustrates: "To have lawsuits at all with one another is defeat [*hḗttēma*] for you . . ."

*Agnoḗma:* "To err through ignorance," not necessarily willfully but through thoughtless heedlessness.

Hebrews 9:7 illustrates: ". . . taking blood which he offers for himself and for the errors [*agnoéma*] of the people."

*Apistía:* "Unbelief," challenging the truthfulness of God and failing to act on his trustworthiness. 1 Timothy 1:13 illustrates: ". . . I received mercy because I had acted ignorantly in unbelief [*apistía*] . . ."

Though this by no means exhausts the list of terms in the New Testament which describe and define sin, we can begin to see not only what sin is and does but how it relates to God. Thus we can begin to form in our minds *a theology of sin.* It could assume a form something like this:

| SIN | AS IT RELATES TO GOD |
|---|---|
| HAMARTIÁ (Sin) | *Missing the very point of life,* which is to know God and the beauty of his plan. |
| ASÉBEIA (Ungodliness) | *Ruling God out of our life and plans*—living as if we owed him nothing. |
| PARAKÓĒ (Disobedience) | *Refusing to listen to God,* as if we knew better than he how life should go. |
| PARÁPTOMA (Offense) | *Being consecrated blunderers,* not necessarily with evil intent but still out of line. |
| PARÁBASIS (Transgression) | *Flouting God's laws* of life in conscious, rebellious contempt of his commands. |
| ANOMÍA (Lawlessness) | *Defiance of God's laws,* as if he had not spoken; living in anarchy against God. |
| HḖTTĒMA (Defeat) | *Accepting defeat* as if there were no available resources in Christ. |
| AGNOḖMA (Ignorant error) | *An ignorant mistake,* not so much willful as stupid, but still in error. |
| APISTÍA (Unbelief) | *Calling God a liar* and acting as if he were an enemy trying to deceive us or somehow selfishly desiring to make us miserable by getting us to do something we won't like. |

## The Savior's Word

Before we leave this study of sin, we must hear directly from the Lord Jesus himself. Since he is the Savior from sin, his should be the final word on the subject. In his earthly life and ministry as recorded in the Gospels, our Lord, while not directly unfolding a doctrinal treatment of sin, nevertheless revealed (1) its nature and reality and (2) his consciousness of being victor over it.

In the Gospel of Luke our Lord illustrates the nature of sin in the story of the Prodigal Son:

> And when he had spent everything, a great famine arose in that country, and he began to be in want. So he went and joined himself to one of the citizens of that country, who sent him into his fields to feed swine. And he would gladly have fed on the pods that the swine ate; and no one gave him anything. But when he came to himself he said, "How many of my father's hired servants have bread enough and to spare, but I perish here with hunger!" (Luke 15:14–17).

By this story Jesus shows us what sin is: going out from the Father's house and living a life remote from God, with everything that means in terms of loss, poverty, and uncleanness.

But Jesus declares his victory over sin in these words spoken to a paralyzed man: "Take heart, my son; your sins are forgiven" (Matt. 9:2); and he also says, "For which is easier, to say, 'Your sins are forgiven,' or to say, 'Rise and walk'?" (Matt. 9:5).

Jesus is fully aware of the alienating power of sin, but at the same time, he is wholly conscious of the overcoming grace and forgiveness of a loving heavenly Father whom he represents in his earthly mission of redemption. This redemptive mission is clearly reflected in the announcement of the angel to Joseph about the coming One: ". . . and you shall call his name Jesus [Lord God/Savior], for he will save his people from their sins" (Matt. 1:21).

## Who Else Can "Fix Sin"?

A simple and beautiful example of the Lord's ability to handle the sin problem is the following story of a young man who clearly understood about sin and the Savior. A basic test of the worth of a religion is what it teaches that God has done to "fix sin," according to Jim Mexican, a twenty-year-old Navajo Indian. Jim used the question about "fixing sin" to defeat representatives of a false religion. The story comes to us from Gordon Fraser, director of Southwestern School of Missions at Flagstaff, Arizona:

> Jim Mexican came to us a year ago as a new believer. He is a Navajo, 6′1″ tall, twenty years old. He attended a government school for five years but admits: "I fool around all time—not learn enough English." He started studying his Bible avidly, and we could hear him downstairs at 5 A.M. sounding out his words.
>
> A few months after he came to us, he walked into the office and said, "Want to go to reservation—see my auntie— These fellows go two by two always bodder her—want to chase them off."
>
> We felt that Jim would be no match for these carefully trained cultists, but we finally yielded to his insistence and let him go for the weekend. We prayed and worried some, but Jim was back on Monday wearing a wide grin.
>
> "How did you make out, Jim?" I asked.
>
> "O.K. I guess. They went away and left my auntie alone. I don't think they come back."
>
> "But what did you tell them?"
>
> "I ask them one question."
>
> "What was that? Usually you have to argue a long time before they leave."
>
> "I ask them, 'How you fellows fix sin?' "
>
> "That would be a rather difficult question for them to answer. What did they say?"
>
> "They say, 'Start out right, live clean life, obey the law of the gospel, just stop sinning, and you be alright.' I tell them, 'Too late, I already a bad sinner. Get in jail five times in six months. How you fellows fix sin like that?' "

"What did they say to that?"

"They jump in pick-up truck and slam door. They say, 'Crazy Indian, don't know nothing.' They go away mad. I just laugh at them."

With renewed perspective on sin and its devastation it seems to me our response should be: "Hallelujah, WHAT A SAVIOR!" and a life of grateful cooperation with the saving work of Jesus Christ in us and through us. "For if while we were enemies we were reconciled to God by the death of his Son, *much more, now that we are reconciled, shall we be saved by his life*" (Rom. 5:10, italics mine).

## II. UNDERSTANDING MAN AND HIS PROBLEMS

Using the inside information God has revealed to us in his Word about the nature of man and how to handle a major problem—the flesh.

# CHAPTER SIX

# Man—As Seen by Man

When we look at the hurting, twisted lives around us, distortions of God's beautiful design for the lives of men, we hurt for them. That is because God has given us some understanding, through our relationship with him and our own experience, of what causes pain. Because we can see that only the Lord Jesus can save them from destroying themselves, we long to impart his redemptive, healing word to their hurting hearts. But in doing so, we wonder what place psychology should have in our thinking and in our approach to men's problems. And it seems to me that men, in attempting to alleviate men's problems and hurts apart from God, have made one futile attempt after another to break through to the central causes of human problems. The result is that secular approaches usually end up merely rearranging symptoms, for the world has no truly remedial answers.

A Christian friend of mine, after getting his Master's degree in psychology, sat in my office one day and said, "Well, I sure learned one thing. Now I see how bankrupt psychology is." And he proceeded to tell me about all the problems it *couldn't* handle. As far as he could see, the only valid uses for psychology were to help the counselor understand human behavior, especially neurotic behavior, and to teach parents how to raise their children. These insights are not insignificant, but *understanding* the problem doesn't necessarily *remedy* it.

At this point I would like to make eminently clear that I am *not* against psychology. I am for anything that can truly help people be free from their hurts and hangups. The Lord knows, and so do I from what I see, that this poor, bleeding race needs all the help it can get. So I'm happy to acknowledge those areas where psychology can really help. But on the other hand, neither do I want to place any unfounded confidence in the practice of psychology. I am not a psychologist, nor can I claim to be any kind of armchair expert on the subject. But in my office I have sat across from too many people, emerging from a psychological or psychiatric counseling experience, who have been badly bruised in the process. They are often more confused than enlightened, more burdened with guilt than free, and far more desperate for peace than they were before they sought help.

As I indicated earlier, many psychologists have been evaluating results and reevaluating the validity of their approaches and methods. In my reading I have come across several psychiatrists who have a genuine honesty and humanitarian desire to help people. And in some cases this desire has caused them to revise or reject some of their traditional approaches and to be openly critical of their own field. So if *they* can take a position of critical analysis without being considered harsh and judgmental, I think we Christians should be allowed the same position, even though we are admittedly biased in favor of redemptive Christian truth. We need to keep the value of psychological approaches while recognizing their limitations, and the greatest limitation psychology has is its lack of truly remedial answers; for the most part it gives no credence to biblical truth about the *fall of man, the flesh, and the reality of satanic forces,* to say nothing of *the redemptive value of life in Christ.*

## Value—And Limitations

I think secular psychiatrists are of all men most to be pitied.

They get all the pain and problems laid on them, but they don't know what to do about them or where to take them. That must be utter frustration. So we are not being condemning, just factual, as we try to analyze where *real* help lies. We need to recognize that there *is* limited value in psychology and that value lies basically in helping us to understand ourselves. Psychologists have studied human nature and have tried to understand why we behave the way we behave, or misbehave the way we misbehave, whichever it is. So we need to use whatever advantage that offers. But we need to recognize that usually they don't know what to do with us after they find out what's wrong. Many times the best they can do (being just factual and honest) is to say, "Well, you poor guy, I feel sorry for you. Go home and try to learn to live with yourself. I don't envy you the process. But go ahead—have fun, if you can." We need to recognize value as well as limitations and then remember that we who know Christ are not stuck with the limitations of psychology.

Let's look briefly at a few of the major schools of thought in the fields of psychological counseling. Our idea here is not primarily to put these disciplines down but simply to be able to retain what is truly valuable and discard what is not genuinely therapeutic. We need to recognize a *false basis for counseling* when we see it and to see how we have all been influenced to some degree by these philosophies. We want to be able to discard any false approaches and seek, instead, a proper basis of counseling.

Here is a layman's view of some of the psychological approaches—probably oversimplified but with the results amply verified by my own observations.

## Freud's Approach

Freud seems to have led us to the conclusion that we can excuse any aberration in our behavior by blaming others: our parents, a repressive religious background, and/or other early influences. Psychoanalysis is the proffered answer, which may go on for years but which never seems to accomplish more than a holding action. Often the recommendation is release of repression which only increases the problem.

I remember clearly one situation in which a man having marital difficulties had been advised by his psychiatrist to have an affair with another woman. I had to try to help him, at the end of the line, to be free from the load of guilt acquired by his adulterous action. Here, at least, Freudian psychology compounded the problem, rather than solving it. So it appears that looking back into the past and seeking escape from its conditioning influences—Freud's way—is a dead-end street; the result is permissiveness, the backdrop of our permissive society. This approach leads to denial of personal responsibility or ability to change to better conduct. This is not God's way.

## Men or Mice?

B. F. Skinner offers another way: that of conditioning man's behavior by training his responses through punishment and reward. His view of man is apparently that he is nothing more than an educated animal who can be manipulated, bred, and controlled by other men. Behavior modification is demonstrable with mice and rats, no doubt, but are we mice or men? Who is to regulate the behavior of the men who regulate other men's behavior? And according to whose standards of behavior?

## Non—Directed Counseling

Then there's Carl Rogers' approach, the verbal-mirror method, in which the counselor simply reflects back the counselee's statements without affirming or denying them. Admittedly, there is some help rendered by simply listening to the counselee's tale of woe, but unless some constructive direction is offered, the value of such counseling is nonexistent or at best short-lived. Rogers' approach assumes that man has within himself all the resources he needs to solve his problems; he only needs a verbal mirror to help him see himself. No outside help from God and his Word are needed. The futility of this approach is patently obvious in light of the Christian view of man.

### A Grain of Truth

We can see the fallacy in each of these philosophies because we understand something of the truth of God. But we need to recognize that in *some* ways Freud is right—our past *can* condition us so that we express the hurt that it inflicts. So he has a point—up to a point. But in Christ we are not stuck with our past history. When Christ comes in, he comes to redeem the life, to make all things new. So if I revert back to "I am emotionally disturbed because my father was a bum," I'm not counting on Christian truth. You recall God's Word in 2 Corinthians: ". . . if any man be in Christ, he is a new creature: old things are passed away; behold, all things are become new. And all things are of God . . ." (2 Cor. 5:17–18*a*, KJV). Sometimes we stop too soon in this verse. There is a conjunction after "all things have become new." It adds "and all things are of God." Why are all things new? Because *God* is in the picture now. Since I have Christ, he is the mediator in my life. Now that I have been reconciled to God through Christ, I have a new source of strength from which to operate. So now I don't have to be stuck with my past history.

This truth is very important to me personally. I come from a broken home. My dad was an alcoholic, was unfaithful to my mother, and deserted his family when I was in my teens. Now, that could mark me for life either one way or the other, couldn't it? Well, it did mark me for life; I learned some very valuable lessons from my dad. Unfortunately, they were all negatives, but I still learned from them how *not* to go. Difficult or ugly things in our past can affect us either way. We can be conditioned either negatively or positively, depending on how we react. I learned *how not to live* from my dad. I got some pointed moral lessons from seeing the devastation his conduct produced in our home, and I wasn't even a Christian at that time. Even in the non-Christian world we don't have to be stuck with the negative effects our circumstances bring us, but as Christians, this is all the more true! Christ, living and reigning in us, makes all things new! We have a clear basis for rejecting much of the Freudian system on the simple Christian premise of 2 Corinthians 5:17.

Now, let's take a look at Skinner's approach: Skinner is also right up to a point. Man *will* respond to the stimuli of punishment and reward, and a lot of people operate on that basis. There is even teaching on punishment and rewards in the Scriptures, isn't there? But these aren't the *only* stimuli that God uses—not even the main ones. Man is much more than an animal; *he is made in the image of God!* And this, by the grace of God and the power of the life of Christ in us, is much deeper motivation than Skinner could ever employ with rats in a maze. We aren't just rats in a maze; we are men! So, though Skinner has a certain basic premise that is right, we have to reject his approach, too, because he, like Freud, doesn't have the whole picture together.

As for Carl Rogers, he is right, as far as he goes. He emphasizes that bombarding a person with well-meaning advice violates his personality by preempting his power of choice. And that has certainly been done many times. Giving advice is like applying Band-Aids to cancer, and it is to be avoided by all means because it ends up merely treating symptoms. But Mr. Rogers fails to recognize that an authoritative Word from God isn't just well-meaning advice. The Bible gives us life-and-death instruction on the way God designed the world to operate, particularly the way he has designed man to function. In that inspired Word, God teaches that even he, sovereign God that he is, will not violate our power of choice. So we have to observe that same rule in counseling and refrain from telling people what to do. God lets us choose, but he also warns us that we will inherit the results of our choices. This is the approach we must take in a counseling ministry. Though we can learn from Carl Rogers, as well as from Freud and Skinner, we also see that God has something to offer that the nondirected approach leaves out: the application of redemptive truth.

# CHAPTER SEVEN

# Man As God Sees Him

Man, through the Fall, has inherited a problem. Though unconscious of the fact, he is operating off-center; his life is revolving around the wrong center. To put it another way, he is like a motor operating without a flywheel—all jumps and jerks, with no steadying force to smooth out his operation. Only when Jesus Christ is allowed to enter his life is there any real possibility of his being restored to the normal operating level on which God originally designed man to function. *Man was designed to operate from the spiritual dynamic of the living God at work in his human spirit.*

## Natural Man

But Adam's repudiation of God's rule in his life left him, and the rest of mankind which followed in his train, operating on a *soulish* level of life, living confidently, or despairingly, in the flesh. So man in his natural state, without God in his life, functions out of the resources of *a distorted mind,* since he does not see things from God's perspective, and *a perverse will* (since he imagines himself to be the captain of his own soul), responding to the whims of his *subjective emotions,* since he reasons that if it "feels good" it must be all right.

We see this documented in the Scripture in such passages as these:

> . . . the natural [literally, *soulish*] man receives not the things of the spirit of God; for they are folly to him . . . (1 Cor. 2:14, literal rendering).

> But we impart [through the word of the cross] a secret and hidden wisdom of God . . . "What no eye has seen, nor ear heard, nor the heart of man conceived [that which is not perceived by the unaided human senses], what God has prepared for those who love him," God has revealed to us through the Spirit. For the Spirit searches everything, even the depths of God (1 Cor. 2:7 and 9–10).

Notice, "What God has prepared . . . God has revealed . . . through the Spirit."

**Number One Need**

It is imperative, therefore, that we introduce those we are endeavoring to help to the saving grace of Jesus Christ. The counselor must do the work of an evangelist, helping his counselee understand what it means to receive Christ and to begin to enjoy the benefit of his indwelling presence through the Spirit. We need to learn to do this in life-related terms, though, so we don't sound like we are just reciting a lot of pious platitudes.

I well remember talking to a young businessman whose life was a shambles. To him the appeal of the gospel needed to be expressed like this: "It appears to me, from what you've told me, that your whole life needs to be under new management." And he agreed. So I simply explained that if he were willing to receive Christ, that *He* would undertake to be the new management, because he is Lord! When he understood the simple proposition that the Lord Jesus was knocking at his door and waiting to be asked into his life, he responded with, "Welcome home, Lord!"

When Christ comes in, he brings with him the whole Godhead, for the Scripture teaches that the Spirit of Christ dwells in every believer and that the Father moves in along with the Son. We see this in Romans and in John:

> . . . Any one who does not have the Spirit of Christ does not belong to him. But if *Christ is in you* . . . your spirits are alive . . . If the *Spirit of him* who raised Jesus from the dead *dwells in you,* he who raised Christ Jesus from the dead will give life to your mortal bodies also through his Spirit which dwells in you (Rom. 8:9–11, *italics mine*).

This Scripture makes it clear that "the Spirit of Christ" in you is synonymous with "Christ in you."

And in our Lord's own words, ". . . If a man loves me, he will keep my word, and my Father will love him, and *we will come to him and make our home with him*" (John 14:23, italics mine). Amazing truth! But reasonable enough when we remember that the three Persons of the Godhead are still *one God.* And if there is the remotest possibility of our gaining all that God is, living in us to transform our situation from a mere existence to *really living,* then we should be quick to respond to such an attractive offer and eager to share this good news. When the gospel is put in all the attractiveness it holds in reality, the response is often, "Sure, I want to receive Christ. Who wouldn't?"

You may be thinking at this point, "How come there are so many mixed-up Christians, if the Spirit of Christ, and all the Godhead, lives in us?" The answer is that receiving Christ is only the *beginning* of a new life, and many Christians have yet to learn, consistently, to *let him be Lord.* In the process of learning we need to know how to deal with our two most formidable enemies: the flesh and the devil. Without understanding that our Lord has provided effective ways to combat these forces, we would all be continually mixed up. The flesh is the enemy within us, while the devil attacks us from the outside. The tactics of our warfare, then, must be specifically related to the enemy. In this chapter we will seek to make clear the means of combating the devil, and in the next chapter we will deal with the devil's masterpiece of subversion—the flesh.

**Public Enemy Number 1**

That old serpent, the devil, deserves the unenviable rating of Public Enemy Number 1. He is called "the accuser of the brethren," and his varied titles run from "The Destroyer" to "The Lord of the Flies." He is the "god of the garbage dump," for all his efforts seem to be directed at putting God down by showing how effectually he can mess up people. We need to know how to cope with man's ancient enemy, for he is a formidable (but defeated) foe.

In these days of the more obvious and overt activities of Satan, we must be sure we know how he can be thwarted. The word of God instructs us to "resist the devil and he will flee from you" (James 4:7). This is an amazing word: The Devil will run away! We are to resist, not in our own strength, but in the power of our risen Lord, who has already defeated this implacable foe—the enemy of our souls:

> And you, who were dead . . . God made alive together with him . . . having canceled the bond which stood against us . . . nailing it to the cross. He disarmed the principalities and powers and made a public example of them, triumphing over them in it [that is, in the cross] (Col. 2:13–15, preferred rendering).

My fellow pastor, Ray Stedman, has expounded Ephesians 6, containing the major passage of this subject most effectively in his book entitled *Spiritual Warfare*, having discovered the key to its application: *"Putting on the armor of God* is simply *putting on Christ,* as our sure defense against defeat." An outline of his more comprehensive treatment follows:

**Strategy of Defense**

> ". . . be strong in the Lord and in the strength of his might. Put on the whole armor of God that you may be able to stand

against the wiles of the devil" (Eph. 6:10–11). (Read Eph. 6:10–17 to see the whole picture.)

## A. Putting on Your Armor (Putting on CHRIST)

1. The Armor You Have Already ("You in Me . . .") (John 14:20*b*).
   - The girdle of *Truth* (Eph. 6:14).
     This is the place to begin. In Christ you have found the key to life, ultimate reality. He *is* the truth—and has told it to us as it really is!

   - The breastplate of *Righteousness* (Eph. 6:14).
     Christ is the ground of our acceptance before God (2 Cor. 5:21). We are "accepted in the Beloved" without qualification or reservation! This guards our hearts—our emotional life.

   - Shoes—the *Good News of Peace* (Eph. 6:15).
     Your feet shod with the readiness produced by the gospel of peace. Peace in the heart makes us ready for the battle, and "He is our peace" (Eph. 2:14).

2. The Armor You Must Take Up ("I in You . . .") (Jn. 14:20*b*). (To be used every time we're attacked)

   - The shield of *Faith* (Eph. 6:16).
     This is believing and acting upon the truth as it is in Jesus. *Faith always anchors to facts.* This is God's ABM system to stop the enemy's guided missiles!

   - The Helmet of *Salvation* (Eph. 6:17).
     Here is protection for the head—and with it the mind—the ability to think and reason. Salvation here is referring to the Lord's ability to rescue us from our current problems as well as his ultimate appearing to set things right, as in 1 Thessalonians 5:1–11 and Romans 8:22–25. Our minds are to be protected by the truth that God *hasn't* lost control of things, and what is happening right NOW is in his plan—to culminate in the full expression of his salvation.

- The Sword of the *Spirit—The Word of God* (Eph. 6:17). This is applying a specific promise or "saying" of God to our own experience, meeting the enemy attack with the specific truth the Spirit of God wants to use to rout him. This is both an offensive and defensive weapon.

  Note, with this we come full circle. Our armor is complete, as it anchors back into the truth. Jesus said, "I AM THE TRUTH" (John 14:6). We start with the truth and end with the truth—surrounded and protected in Christ who *is* the truth.

B. THE FINAL WORD—PRAY

"Pray at all times in the Spirit, with all prayer and supplication. To that end keep alert with all perseverance . . ." (Eph. 6:18*a*).

Prayer, the ultimate expression of our dependence, is the final word that ties our strategy of defense all together. In our prayer, we need to be "making supplication for all the saints . . ." (Eph. 6:18*b*). In the realm of spiritual warfare, perhaps more than any other, it becomes evident that we need to pray for each other, often corporately, for though the devil is a defeated enemy, he is a terrible foe, fighting a last-ditch battle. We need to take our Lord's prayer often upon our lips, "Father . . . I do not pray that thou shouldst take them out of the world, but that thou shouldst keep them from the evil one" (John 17:15). In other words, we are praying, "Don't remove them from the place of danger, just keep them from the enemy's power in the midst of it."

## CHAPTER EIGHT

# The Enemy Within

If the devil is Public Enemy Number 1, the flesh certainly qualifies as Public Enemy Number 2. One of the most useful areas of counseling is helping people learn to deal with what the Bible calls "the flesh." This is a realm in which only God, not psychology, has any information. It is only the Bible that instructs us on this major problem in mankind. So, as God's people, we need to find out all we can about the subject.

First, let's seek to define the flesh. How do you understand the term? One group I asked came up with these ideas: Self, acting apart from God; doing what comes naturally; a drive to be separate from God; a valiant attempt to make a go of it without God; self-sufficiency; doing as you please without reference to God. Note that most of these definitions share the common factor of leaving God out, and that is the essential idea.

Here are some of my own attempts to define the flesh:

1) That evil tendency in man to try to leave God out and try to go it alone.

2) The spirit of independence that cuts God out of thoughts and actions.

3) Our basic fallen humanness proceeding from Adam, characterized by a fancied independence from God.

4) The inherent tendency to trust in one's self rather than in God.

5) The seat of the rebel spirit that resists the control of

God in the life. (It includes the *best,* as well as the *worst* that man can do without God. It also includes all those neat, respectable sins, those refined types of sin that we protect. Incidentally, the flesh can be very religious, often putting up a front of relating to God while actually resisting God.)

## Identifying the Flesh

We can use several approaches in learning to identify the flesh at work, in ourselves or someone else:

1) Examine the source of your thought processes. Are you exhibiting earthly or heavenly wisdom?
2) Compare Galatians 5:19 and 5:22, 23, contrasting the works of the flesh and the fruit of the Spirit. See which one fits.
3) Examine some of the biblical illustrations like Abraham, Esau, Jacob, and Amalek.
4) Check through some of the common forms of rationalizing—ways of excusing fleshly activities or thought patterns.

Let's look at each of these in more detail.

## Two Kinds of Wisdom

One way to identify the flesh is to examine the *source* of our thought processes. James has a good word on the subject:

> Who is wise and understanding among you? By his good life let him show his works in the meekness of wisdom. But if you have bitter jealousy and selfish ambition in your hearts, do not boast and be false to the truth. This wisdom is not such as comes down from above, but is earthly, unspiritual, devilish. For where jealousy and selfish ambition exist, there will be disorder and every vile practice. But the wisdom from above is first pure, then peaceable, gentle, open to reason, full of mercy and good fruits, without uncertainty or insincerity. And the harvest of righteousness is sown in peace by those who make peace (James 3:13–18).

This penetrating passage highlights two kinds of wisdom,

deriving from two different sources. So we ask ourselves, "Where am I getting my information? Where are my thought processes coming from?" One way to recognize the flesh, then, is to identify the source of our attitudes and behavior, using James' helpful checklist outlined below:

| WISDOM FROM ABOVE | THE OTHER KIND |
|---|---|
| • Pure<br>• Gentle<br>• Open to Reason<br>• Full of Mercy<br>• Full of Good Fruits<br>• Without Uncertainty<br>• Without Insincerity<br>• Producing a Harvest of Righteousness—a Good Life. | is marked by:<br><br>• Bitter Jealousy<br>• Selfish Ambition<br>• Boasting<br>• Being False to the Truth<br><br>is being:<br><br>• Earthly<br>• Unspiritual<br>• Devilish<br>• Producing Disorder and Every Vile Practice. |

**Observe the Results**

Another way is to carefully observe the *results* of our actions and attitudes. Galatians 5:19–21 tells us the results of operating in the flesh:

> Now the works of the flesh are plain: immorality, impurity, licentiousness, idolatry, sorcery, enmity, strife, jealousy, anger, selfishness, dissension, party spirit, envy, drunkenness, carousing, and the like.

We all like to hurry through this list. We don't like to look too closely at these words. But if we're willing to face the music, we will ask: Are my actions producing *strife* or *dissension,* or *anger?* If so, what is the source? It is the flesh. If we go on, continuing through the whole rotten list, we can identify the problem and its source.

On the other hand, Galatians 5:22 tells us: "The fruit of the Spirit is love, joy, peace, patience, kindness, goodness, faithfulness, gentleness, self-control." The vivid contrast between the works of the flesh and the fruit of the Spirit helps us to identify clearly the basis of our actions, whether it is the flesh or the Spirit.

## Biblical Examples

Another way to pinpoint the flesh in action is to look at some of the illustrations in the characters of the Bible. The first one who comes to my mind is Abraham. That may sound strange, since we generally think of Abraham as the *man of faith.* But Abraham had his lapses, even as we do. One in particular, far-reaching in its effects, is recorded in Genesis 16.

Abraham, on the advice of Sarah, decided that he should have a son by Hagar, Sarah's maid. The problem was that God hadn't come through on his promise to send Abraham and Sarah a son, so they said, "Lord, you need our help. If you can't make it, we'll help you out." The significance of their action comes dramatically to light when you think about the implications of circumcision, instituted by God, following Abraham's decision to help God out (Genesis 17). Circumcision is a cutting off of the flesh of the sex organ, and the sex organ was the instrument that Abraham decided to use to do God's work for him. Connect this with Colossians 2:11 and you can see what God was teaching in circumcision: "In him [that is, in Christ] also you were circumcized with a circumcision made without hands, by putting off the body of flesh in the circumcision of Christ."

Now the result of this fleshly union was Ishmael, and "Ishmael" has been a problem to "Isaac" throughout history, and still is today. In the Middle East we see two opposing forces right across the border from each other *still fighting*—and this is the result of Abraham's fleshly lapse. To me that is a very potent illustration of how crucial our decisions are and how clear it is that we should let God fulfill his own promises instead of trying to help him out by our fleshly maneuvers.

It is easy for us to see the flesh at work in Abraham and Sarah, but it is amazing how hard it is to see it in ourselves. For we do the same thing. We're no different. Did you ever get impatient about God's apparent slowness in keeping his promises? That's the same idea. We rationalize our impatience, saying, "We just want to hurry up the process." But every time we get impatient, we are saying the same thing Abraham and Sarah did: "Lord, you are not making it. But that's all right—we will help you out. Just watch us, we'll get results!" And of course the results we get are exactly like theirs.

## Twin Pictures

Another illustration of the flesh at work—actually a double picture—is the story of Jacob and Esau, who were twin brothers. Esau pictures the flesh in the *unbeliever* (and he was the more appealing of the two, from a human viewpoint), while Jacob, the little sniveling wretch, was a picture of the flesh in the *believer*—a rather pointed shot at us who are believers.

Esau disdained his spiritual inheritance and sold it for a plate of bean soup! That's a pretty cheap price, even when you are hungry. Thus Esau ruled God out entirely, judging him to be of no importance in his life. Jacob, on the other hand, valued the spiritual inheritance, and really did his best to gain it, but he went about it the wrong way. God had already made up his mind that Jacob was to have the inheritance, but Jacob was a schemer, and he decided to get it *his* way, not God's. (The story of Jacob's deception is in Gen. 27.)

Nevertheless, this devious Jacob, whose name means "supplanter," became Israel, which means "prince with God." When Jacob finally accepted God as sovereign in his life, God changed his name to reflect the nature and purpose he had planned all along for Jacob to have and fulfill.

## War with Amalek

Later on, in Exodus 17, we find the story of Amalek, who further illustrates the work of the flesh, clearly portraying God's attitude toward it:

> Then came Amalek and fought with Israel at Rephidim. And Moses said to Joshua, "Choose for us men, and go out, fight with Amalek; tomorrow I will stand on the top of the hill with the rod of God in my hand." So Joshua did as Moses told him, and fought with Amalek; and Moses, Aaron, and Hur went up to the top of the hill. Whenever Moses held up his hand, Israel prevailed; and whenever he lowered his hand, Amalek prevailed. But Moses' hands grew weary; so they took a stone and put it under him, and he sat upon it, and Aaron and Hur held up his hands, one on one side, and the other on the other side; so his hands were steady until the going down of the sun. And Joshua mowed down Amalek and his people with the edge of the sword. And the Lord said to Moses, "Write this as a memorial in a book and recite it in the ears of Joshua, that I will utterly blot out the remembrance of Amalek from under heaven." And Moses built an altar and called the name of it, The Lord is my banner, saying, "A hand upon the banner of the Lord! The Lord will have war with Amalek from generation to generation" (Ex. 17:8–16).

Here is a beautifully pictorial representation of the battle against the flesh. Amalek was Esau's grandson, descended from the same fleshly line. God was taking the Israelites into the land of promise. (Israel, the nation, is a picture of the believer, and the land of promise represents the spiritual victory we are meant to enjoy.) Amalek is a picture of the flesh, the force designed to thwart God's desire to give us spiritual victory. The flesh constantly fights against what God wants—our living in triumph in Christ.

As we follow through this remarkable picture of our spiritual life, we must remember that the children of Israel had come from Egypt, and they had crossed the Red Sea (which is a picture of our commitment to Christ—cutting off the way back). Moses was to take them all the way into the land of promise (the place of spiritual victory). But Amalek (picturing the flesh) tried to keep them out, opposing the entrance of Israel into the land of promise. In the same way, in our lives, the flesh always opposes God's program for spiritual victory.

In this story, the rod is the symbol of power, the authority of faith—and when it was held up, the Israelites won. The battle didn't depend on fighting, it depended on *faith*—even though there was indeed fighting going on. But who was doing the fighting? It was Joshua, and the name Joshua is the Hebrew equivalent of "Jesus." So in our lives, who does the fighting? It is always Jesus; our part in the battle against the flesh is simply to believe.

After the battle was won, we read in verse 14, "And the Lord said to Moses, 'Write this as a memorial in a book and recite it in the ears of Joshua, that I will utterly blot out the remembrance of Amalek from under heaven.' " What Moses was to write down constituted what would later be included in the law of the Jews. And since Joshua is a representation of Jesus, what the Lord is saying here, in effect, is that the law (what Moses was given to write down) is to communicate a directive to Jesus ("recite it in the ears of Joshua"). The content of that directive is that God will, through Jesus, "utterly blot out the remembrance of Amalek from under heaven." Jesus, in other words, was sent into the world to deal effectively and authoritatively with the flesh—not only once, but for all time: "The Lord will have war with Amalek from generation to generation." This Old Testament story is therefore a graphic portrayal of the commitment of the Lord Jesus to faithfully and continuously deal with the flesh in our lives.

## Getting Values Straight

One last biblical example is the Apostle Paul's attitude, in which we can learn an essential fact concerning the nature of the flesh but one which is particularly hard for us to recognize in ourselves:

> For we are the true circumcision, who worship God in spirit, and glory in Christ Jesus, and put no confidence in the flesh. Though I myself have reason for confidence in the flesh also. If any other man thinks he has reason for confidence in the flesh, I have more: circumcised on the eighth day, of the people of Israel, of the tribe of Benjamin, a Hebrew born of Hebrews; as to the law a Pharisee, as to zeal a persecutor of the church, as to righteousness under the law blameless. But whatever gain I had, I counted as loss for the sake of Christ. Indeed I count everything as loss because of the surpassing worth of knowing Christ Jesus my Lord. For his sake I have suffered the loss of all things, and count them as refuse, in order that I may gain Christ and be found in him, not having a righteousness of my own, based on law, but that which is through faith in Christ, the righteousness from God that depends on faith (Phil. 3:3–9).

Do you see what he is saying? Paul counted his ancestry, his education, his religious heritage, and his personal righteousness all as worthless garbage in view of the surpassing worth of knowing Christ. Therein lay his victory over the flesh. He chose to reject all the things that the world values highly as being of no worth in terms of where he placed his confidence. Paul had plenty of reasons to take pride in himself, however. He was a brilliant man, an able student, a well-instructed scholar of the truth of God. He was a Pharisee, a "fundamentalist of the fundamentalists" of his day. Yet he was able to say, "We put no confidence in the flesh."

For us, it's comparatively easy to recognize the obviously negative things in our lives as fleshly—things like jealousy, strife, and the like. But to pride ourselves in educational prowess or mental brilliance—that's fleshly, too. If you were to somehow suddenly be stripped of all your educational background, or to discover that your great-grandparents didn't come over on the Mayflower after all, or to learn that your career was henceforth rendered meaningless by some technological advance, would you crumble? Take a look and see where your confidence really lies. It may startle you, but it will free you to begin to depend more totally on the One who is totally dependable.

Paul had his values straight. He got his insight the hard way, however, by being blinded for a few days so he could finally see the truth. These words of his are well worth remembering: "We are the circumcision." Circumcision is always a picture of the cutting off of the flesh—spiritual circumcision (of the heart, not of the body). Thus it pictures putting aside any confidence in ourselves. "The circumcision" are further described as those "who worship God in spirit." Worship is "worthship," and Christians are those who have discovered that *real* worth is in God, not in us. Furthermore, those who have circumcized hearts "glory in Christ Jesus." But how? By placing our confidence in him as our indwelling Lord.

## Truth in Labeling

There is one more way we can identify the flesh, and that is to recognize some of the ways in which we rationalize our carnal attitudes. Here are a few typical rationalizations:

Others have *prejudices,* but we have *convictions.*
Others are *conceited,* but in me it's *self-respect.*
Others are *social-climbing snobs,* but with me it's *just trying to get ahead.*

If you are unyielding about your views of Scripture, that's *just plain stubbornness;* but in me, it's *contending for the faith.*

When you spend time on your personal appearance, it's *vanity;* in me, it's *just making the most of my God-given assets.*

In you, it's *impatience;* while in me, it's *"have you noticed how annoying everyone is?"*

In you, it's *touchiness;* but in me, it's *sensitivity.*

In you, it's *self-righteousness;* while in me it's amply justified, because *I really am right.*

In you, it's *worry;* in me, *concern.*

In you, it's *self-justification;* but in me it's just *explaining my position.*

In you, it's a *bad temper;* while I "blew my stack" because *they had it coming and I couldn't let them get away with it.*

Do you see how this works? It's a pretty familiar process, isn't it? But in order to deal with the flesh in us, as we will work through in a moment, we must first label it for what it is. Perhaps the following summary list will be helpful.

Various Forms and Expressions of SELF:

- Self-approbation
- Self-justification
- Self-indulgence
- Self-pleasing
- Self-reliance
- Self-effort
- Self-centeredness
- Self-righteousness
- Self-pity
- Self-protectiveness
- Self-assertiveness
- Self-confidence

*Then there's:* selfish ambition, stubbornness, bigotry, false modesty, anxiety, withdrawal, hypersensitivity, impatience, egotism, inferiority feelings, vanity, hostility, nervousness, depression, a critical spirit, dominance, indifference, fear, guilt, avarice, lovelessness, dissension, envy, pride—and YOU NAME IT!

If you consider each one carefully you will see how all of these traits simply rule God out of our scene and leave us shut up to our own human resources. And as has been said, "A man wrapped up in himself makes a mighty small package."

# CHAPTER NINE

# Death and Freedom

It's clear now, I hope, that the works of the flesh are sin. But unless we understand their effects in human life—the devastation that results—we won't have the full picture nor the motivation we need to truly help those who are in bondage to the flesh.

Remember, man was made to operate with Christ reigning in his spirit; that's the normal Christian life. Man is designed to be the temple of God, with God enjoying his rightful place in the temple, the place of worship. Worship means that in every situation God proves to be *worth* something to us. If he doesn't, we are not worshiping, and he is out of that place of worship. Whenever Christ is not reigning in the life, man reverts to operating out of a soul-level of life, not from the control center, which is the Spirit.

Paul, coming to a conclusion on this whole subject, says: "So then, brethren, we are debtors, not to the flesh, to live according to the flesh—*for if you live according to the flesh you will die,* but if by the Spirit you put to death the deeds of the body you will live" (Rom. 8:12–13, italics mine).

Looking at the local context, examine this eighth chapter of Romans up to the thirteenth verse, underlining the word *flesh,* and you will see that it appears thirteen times in thirteen verses. So it is obvious that Paul has in mind to give us the facts about the flesh. Then, if you put a circle around the word Spirit whenever it occurs, you will find that this word appears an almost equal number of times. So it seems clear that Paul wants us to understand about living according to the flesh and life in the Spirit. To examine just one instance, verse nine says: "But you are not in the flesh, you are in the Spirit, if the Spirit of God really dwells in you."

God has in mind our need to operate in an entirely different sphere of life, which is implicit in this verse. We have been taken out of the Adamic realm of operation and placed into the Christian realm. He says flatly, "You are not in the flesh." Now it's true that the flesh may be dominant in us at times, but we are not *in* the flesh if we belong to Christ. Do you see the difference? And if we lapse back into the flesh, we will die a little as the result of that temporary fleshly fling.

In this verse it seems clear that Paul is dealing with Christians—those in whom the Spirit of God lives. The "if" is not truly conditional here but could better be translated "since." To confirm this, when we get to verse twelve, he says, "Brethren," and brethren are Christians, so there is no doubt whom he is addressing here, is there? "*We* are debtors" (here he includes himself) "not to the flesh, to live according to the flesh, for if *you* [notice, he has changed the pronoun from "we" to "you" since he has already decided not to live according to the flesh] live according to the flesh you will die." He is not speaking here of losing our salvation, but of dying. But how will we die? Here's what I think he is telling us.

## Sin Pays Wages: Death

Have you ever said, "This thing is killing me?" That slang expression reflects Paul's idea exactly. Some emotional problem, we say, is "killing us." And it *is,* isn't it? When we operate in the flesh, we are actually losing out in some aspect of life. That's what Paul is talking about. This is what is so devastating about the flesh. The reason the Lord is so serious about our dealing with it effectively, is that *it kills us,* whether we are Christians or non-Christians.

When we are not experiencing the abundance of life that Christ came to give us, then we get what always accompanies absence of life—*death.* Death in the non-Christian is total, for he is wholly unresponsive to God. "You who were *dead* in trespasses and sins," Paul says in Ephesians 2, speaking of the Ephesian Christians before they knew Christ. But a Christian can be operating in the flesh and the result is just as deadly as in the non-Christian; it produces the same results—*death,* because life is only experienced in the one who is our life, that is, in Christ. It is only as we allow him to prevail as Lord in our lives that we experience that abundance of life which he came to bring us. So, as you can see, the options are very real, and the flesh is devastating in whomever it functions. See how clearly the Lord spells it out through the Apostle Paul in his letter to the Romans:

> For I know that nothing good dwells within me, that is, in my flesh (Rom. 7:18).
>
> For God has done what the law, weakened by the flesh, could not do (Rom. 8:3).
>
> To set the mind on the flesh is death (Rom. 8:6).
>
> For the mind that is set on the flesh is hostile to God; it does not submit to God's law, indeed it cannot (Rom. 8:7).
>
> Those who are in the flesh cannot please God (Rom. 8:8).
>
> For if you live according to the flesh you will die (Rom. 8: 13).

So it's not surprising that he adds, by way of conclusion: "*Put on the Lord Jesus Christ,* and *make no provision* for the flesh, to gratify its desires" (Rom. 13:14, italics mine).

## Facts about the Flesh

What the Lord wants to do is spare us the kind of pain and death that inevitably results from operating in the flesh. Let's consider each of these Scriptures one by one: "For I know that nothing good dwells in me, that is my flesh"

(Rom. 7:18). Do you believe that? Most people don't, you know. The non-Christian doesn't believe it, and many times we Christians don't either. Paul was saying this about himself, and I suggest that if it was true of him, it's true of you and me, too.

In Romans 8:3: "For God has done what the law, weakened *by the flesh* could not do." What did God do that the law couldn't do? He gave us the capacity to fulfill the requirements of the law, to live righteously. The flesh, that is, our dependence on our own ability, was what kept the law from accomplishing true righteousness. To put this in its setting: Romans 7 is the admission of failure to achieve—the key feature is: "What I want to do I don't do; what I don't want to is what I end up doing." That is utter frustration, part of the devastation of the flesh.

"The mind set *on the flesh* is death" (Rom. 8:6). This verse says that if we think in accordance with a fleshly approach to life, we are going to experience death. Expanding on his point, Paul continues, "For the mind that is set *on the flesh* is hostile to God; it does not submit to God's law, indeed it cannot" (Rom. 8:7, italics mine). This tells us there is no way the flesh can perform in fellowship with God. It is hostile to God and it *cannot* submit to what God has in mind. Very assertive and dogmatic statements, aren't they? "What is *your* mind-set?" is a question I often ask.

Finally, "Those who are *in the flesh* cannot please God" (Rom. 8:8, italics mine). Here we must ask, who are "those who are in the flesh"? Is it not the non-Christian? The flesh is the sphere in which he functions; it's all he knows. This brings us back to our first responsibility as counselors to non-Christians: Help them to know Christ, so they will have a better world to live in—the world of the Spirit.

## Enjoying Life

Now we are ready to turn the corner and discover the way

to freedom from the flesh. Christ came to bring us LIFE, and in chapter thirteen of Romans there is this very important statement: "Put on the Lord Jesus Christ, and make no provision *for the flesh,* to gratify its desires" (Rom. 13:14, italics mine). God wants us to make no allowance for indulging the flesh. If we believe it's possible to do this and see the high stakes that are involved, then we will begin to be sensible and learn to live in accordance with all that God has made available to us in the Lord Jesus. Notice the positive and negative: "put on the Lord Jesus Christ," that's the positive; and "make no provision for the flesh to gratify its desires," the negative!

A man told me not long ago, "I pray about this matter of my attitude all day long and still don't gain victory." Here is a place where prayer is totally ineffectual, but not because God is unfaithful. In this case it was because this man was making provision for the flesh; it was a smokescreen. My reply to him was, "Did you ever think that maybe the Lord is saying to you, *"Don't talk to me about it, I've already talked to you about it?"* So often that is what the Lord has to say to all of us: "I've told you how to deal with it. Now, do it! Don't try to fake me out with words; just do what I have told you!" Isn't it atrocious how deceitful we are? This man was utterly sincere; he was just as open and non-defensive as he could be; he wasn't trying to cover up, but he didn't understand what the flesh was doing to him.

Earlier in our conversation he had said bitterly, "I could kill my mother. She's the one who ruined me." What does that say about his problem? What manifestation of the flesh is this? Blaming someone else for my problem becomes a means of justification, does it not? And as long as I'm trying to blame another for my failure, the real problem can never be solved. Sure, his mother had wronged him, but he doesn't have to be stuck with that. Paul said, ". . . if any one is in Christ, he is a new creation; the old has passed away, behold, the new has come" (2 Cor. 5:17). New deal!

What this illustration shows is how devilish and deceiving the flesh is. And I dare say all of us have one or more areas where we demonstrate the same kind of blind spot as this man did. Indeed, one of the most subtle and damaging ways we reveal that we are operating in the flesh is to express confidence that we are walking in the Spirit. A young man walked into my office one day and said, "I've learned to walk in the Spirit 80 percent of the time." I said, "It's not the 80 percent we're worried about! It's the other 20 percent!" Spirituality is like humility—when you brag about it, you've already lost it!

**Freed from Slavery**

The way to render the flesh inoperative (what a marvelous prospect!) is to *judge it.* That's how the job gets done! You see, God has *already* judged the flesh IN CHRIST. What we must do is to agree with him that the "old man" is dead and has no right to try to assert himself in us. Romans 6 tells the way it works:

1. YOU DIED WITH CHRIST.
   "For we know that *our old man was crucified with Him* so that the body as it was characterized by sin might be put out of work and *we might no longer be enslaved to sin"* (Rom. 6:6, literal rendering).
   This is GOD'S EMANCIPATION PROCLAMATION—and the key word is "know." We start by *knowing* this FACT: I am identified with Christ in his death—so *I died with Christ,* in God's reckoning.

2. COUNT ON IT.
   "So also all of you [as with Christ] reckon yourselves to be dead to sin and alive to God" (Rom. 6:11, literal rendering).
   "Reckon" is the word here. This is the step of FAITH—believing the FACT. God has *said* it—now I *believe* it!
   Incidentally, "dead" here means "unresponsive to," or *separated from the necessity of responding to the "old man."*

3. GO FREE.
"Stop yielding your members as instruments of unrighteousness to sin, but yield yourselves to God, *as men who have been brought out of death to life,* and your members as instruments of righteousness to God" (Rom. 6:13, literal rendering).

True liberty is being what God designed us to be—instruments of his grace. Now since our *old man died with Christ,* we have the liberty to choose to serve God—to be his men and women. So the key word here is YIELD.

We gain victory over the flesh as we:

| KNOW ............ RECKON ............ YIELD |
|---|

Then we can walk in newness of life ". . . for since we have been united with him in conformity to his death, so also we shall be in his resurrection" (Rom. 6:5, freely rendered). The chart on page 92 shows how it works.

## True Liberation

The Christians' heritage through the saving work of Christ is to be freed from slavery to sin and to live like kings, because we are the royal residence of the KING! For ". . . those who receive the abundance of grace [all the resources and ability of our risen Lord] and the free gift of righteousness [right standing with God—full acceptance before him] *reign in life* through the one man Jesus Christ" (Rom. 5:17*b,* italics mine). This is a description of the normal Christian life—God's provision for *every one* of his own, not just for super-saints!

The apostle supports this truth on the other side with, ". . . sin will have no dominion over you, since you are not under law but under grace" (Rom. 6:14). Grace supplies what law never could; a Savior who died for us—*that he*

# HOW TO LIVE LIKE A KING . . .
## instead of a slave.

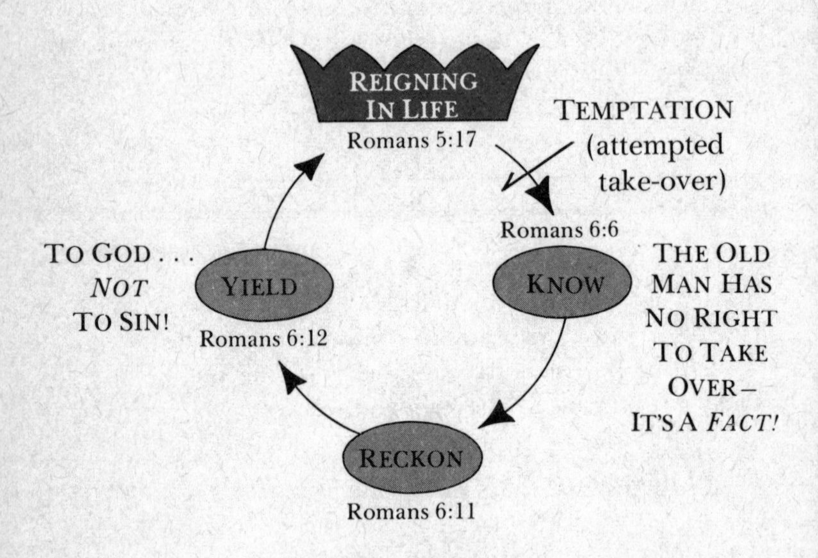


COUNT ON IT,
BECAUSE IT'S TRUE–
FOR *THIS* SITUATION.

We take this ATTITUDE: "Always carrying in the body the dying of Jesus, so that the life of Jesus may also be manifested in our bodies"
2 Corinthians 4:10.

*might live in us!* "Indeed, since we died with Christ, we believe that we shall live with him" (Rom. 6:8, a literal rendering); ". . . so that as Christ was raised from the dead by the glory of the Father, we too might walk in newness of life" (Rom. 6:4*b*). Do you see the implications of this truth? We are no longer enslaved by sin!

If I had been a slave when Abraham Lincoln, as President of the United States, issued his Emancipation Proclamation, I believe I would have carried a copy of that document wherever I went, even if I couldn't read it. Then if some rednecked sheriff had laid his hands on me and said, "Hey, boy, you're a slave," I would have flashed the proclamation and replied, "No sir, I'm free!"

That's exactly what God wants us to do when sin tries to take us captive. We can say, "I'm free! When Christ died, 'Old Bob' died. I refuse to accept those old shackles! I'm going to live like a king!" To me it's nothing short of inspiration that chooses the opposing figures of *slavery* and *kingship* to display the high value of the liberty we have in Jesus Christ. For who wants to be a slave? And who wouldn't want to "live like a king"? Public Enemy Number 2 is a defeated foe, through him who loved us and gave himself for us—and *to* us.

## The Theory Applied

You may be saying, "Sounds like good theory, but how does it work?" Let's look at an example. Often, in counseling, I find that Christians are beset with inferiority feelings. This is always the result of comparing themselves with others and coming out second-best in their own estimation. Evaluating their worth in this way is an example of the flesh because it totally ignores God and his Word on this subject.

If we turn to check out God's viewpoint on our worth we get information like this:

> . . . with me it is a very small thing that I should be judged by you or by any human court. I do not even judge myself. I am not aware of anything against myself, but I am not thereby acquitted. It is the Lord who judges me. Therefore do not pronounce judgment before the time, before the Lord comes, who will bring to light the things now hidden in darkness and will disclose the purposes of the heart. Then every man will receive his commendation from God (1 Cor. 4:3–5).

Notice it says *commendation,* not *condemnation,* because for the Christian "there is therefore now no condemnation" (Rom. 8:1). I have no business making inept and unfounded comparisons—from which feelings of inferiority flow—and, therefore, I have no business feeling inferior. I just need to be a faithful steward of all that God entrusts to me regardless of what anyone else does, as the context of this passage declares: ". . . it is required of stewards that they be found trustworthy" (1 Cor. 4:2).

I love the Apostle Paul's handling of this problem of comparisons, as recorded later in the Corinthian letters. He was being compared (unfavorably, it seems) with other preachers by the Corinthian believers. In his response he said, with subtle irony, "I regard myself not the least inferior to your super-apostles" (2 Cor. 11:5, freely translated). Do you see how completely he dealt with any possible feelings of inferiority (or superiority, for that matter)? He just refused to acknowledge that there was any competition, knowing that the ministries of various Christians are *cooperative,* not competitive. That's the whole point of the church being the body of Christ. As with our human bodies, so in the church the various members cooperate rather than compete with one another. In commenting on the sheer folly of making comparisons, Paul had this to say: "Not that we venture to class or compare ourselves with some of those who commend themselves. But when they measure themselves by one another, and compare themselves with one another, they are without understanding" (2 Cor. 10:12).

What a wonderfully liberating word this is. God says, "Inferiority, what's that? Who's comparing?" And the whole matter is settled. The flesh is put in its place—on the cross with Christ and I'm saved from all kinds of related problems like self-pity, self-protectiveness, depression, anxiety, and so forth. We are not indebted to the flesh or held captive by it, if we choose to act in accord with God's emancipation proclamation.

So the process of judging the flesh—in this case, feelings of inferiority—is first to *know* what God has to say about our worth and why comparisons have no validity in the kingdom of God. Then, we must believe what God has said, *counting* on his word as truth, and finally, turning our back on the sin. We must give ourselves over once more to the control of Christ in our lives—*yielding* to him and not to the feelings of inferiority.

## Futility–Or Fulfillment?

I have learned to correlate the term "death" with frustration and futility, and the word "life" with fulfillment. The life that Christ came to bring us is not just heaven-by-and-by, but it is *fulfillment* here and now, and heaven later—adding up to total fulfillment all the way. The contrast of these terms is very significant, and it makes *life* very desirable. I like what I know about Jesus Christ, the life he has given me, and all that he unfolds to me day by day. It's from this kind of a thankful, appreciative understanding of the astounding advantage we have as Christians in terms of *really living* that we're able to share the wealth with whomever the Lord put on our program in our counseling ministry.

## III. THE THERAPY OF REDEMPTIVE TRUTH

Making men whole (including ourselves) through the application of God's redemptive Word. Dealing with the major issues of life in ways that make life worth living.

## CHAPTER TEN

# Spirit, Soul, and Body

Man is made up of three parts; he is a tri-unity—like God. He is comprised of *body, soul,* and *spirit.* The Greek word for body is *soma;* soul is *psuche,* from which we get "psyche," and spirit is *pneuma.* We need to observe the relationship of these three parts of man in counseling so as to more easily identify the source of the problem. The body we can easily identify. It is the realm of *world-consciousness,* the seat of the five senses with which we make contact with the world around us. The soul and spirit are not quite so easily distinguishable, but the Scripture makes it clear they are distinct and different: "For the word of God is living and active, sharper than any two-edged sword, piercing to the division of soul and spirit . . ." (Heb. 4:12*a*).

Without wanting to be arbitrary, but still endeavoring to make a distinction between soul and spirit, I find the following definitions to be helpful, even though, admittedly, there seem to be areas in which soul and spirit blend and/or overlap. This is particularly true when we observe that our mind, emotions, and will function both in the realm of the spirit and of the soul. If we keep in mind the fact that there always remains an element of mystery about these distinctions, seeking to define soul and spirit still has practical value. So this is what I've settled on: The soul is the realm of *self-consciousness* and is composed of *mind, emotions, and will.* The spirit is the realm of *God-consciousness.* The spirit of man is designed to be the place where God lives and reigns.

## Where Does It Hurt?

In any counseling situation it is necessary to discover in which of these areas lies the *cause* of the problem. We Christians are sometimes prone to leap to the conclusion that there must be a *spiritual* problem, so we respond to the problem in specifically spiritual terms. But if the problem is originating in *the body,* then it is wrong and/or ineffectual to try to treat the spirit.

For instance, there has recently come into focus a physical deficiency known by the medical profession as hypoglycemia, or low blood sugar. Several people in our immediate Christian family have it. It has definite psychological effects, but it is a *bodily* malfunction. Therefore, it is folly for us to try to treat the matter as a psychological or spiritual problem when it stems from the body. We may be able to give spiritual encouragement which will strengthen our counselee, but we should also ask him to see a medical doctor who can treat the *body.*

## Psychosomatic Illness

You have heard of *psychosomatic* ills, I'm sure. The word "psychosomatic" is an English language combination of two Greek words—*psuche* and *soma.* It thus describes a bodily ailment that is caused by maladjustment in the *soul-life* (or originating from a mental or emotional problem, whichever way you want to put it). A psychologist friend of mine tells me that modern medicine estimates that between 70 and 90 percent of all the illnesses doctors see are psychosomatic rather than physiological in origin. That is obviously a very high percentage, if the statistic is correct. Now, a psychosomatic illness is very real; it isn't just an *imagined* illness, but it stems from a soulish cause–originating in the soul, not in the body.

*DIAGRAM A*

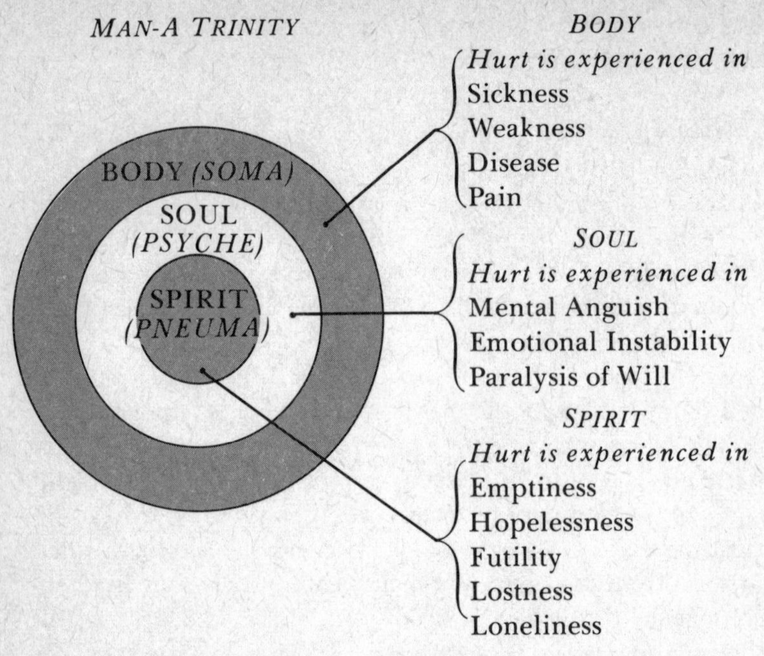


The *SOURCE* of the problem may be in any of these three realms, but the *HURT* affects the *WHOLE PERSON.*

**Pneumosomatic Dis-ease**

I have coined a word to describe another kind of illness. It is *pneumosomatic*. That is, if there is not right adjustment in the spiritual realm, the whole man is affected—in the *soul* and the *body*—although the source of the problem is spiritual. Through counseling on a *spiritual* level I have seen people change both *emotionally* and *physically*. Diagram A may help us to visualize this.

I remember one girl who came to see me with a terrible back problem. She was in such excruciating pain that she couldn't sit still. She kept trying to ease her neck, as she

*DIAGRAM B*

The SPIRITUAL MAN

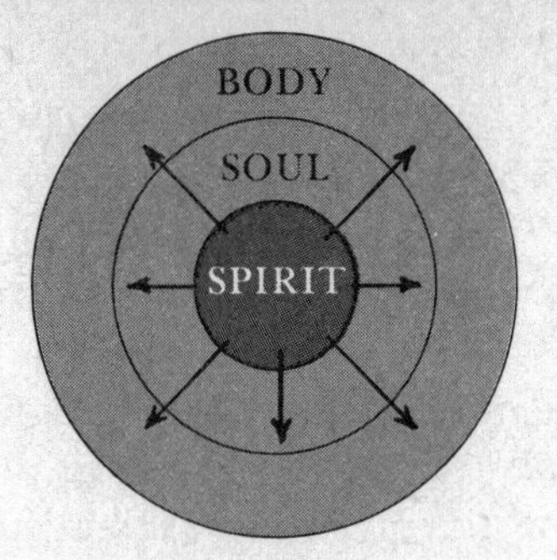


*The Normal Christian Life*
Man indwelt and empowered by the Spirit of God—every area of life affected, body soul & spirit—everything in balance.

The FLESHLY MAN

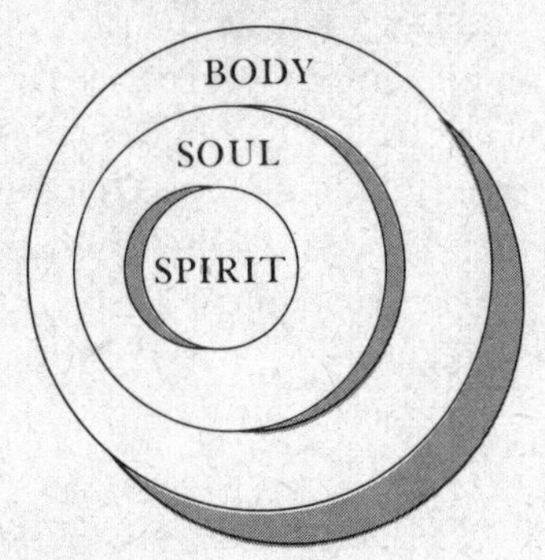


*Off-center—Eccentric*
Life revolving around the wrong center, dominated by his soul (the way he *feels*, *thinks*, and *wills* without including God.)

squirmed and twisted in her chair. As we talked, it became apparent that her deepest problem was not physical, but spiritual. She was blaming God for her illness. I was able to help her see that God had no interest in torturing her and that he really loved her. She began to see that in her despair she was blaming the very One who was the most concerned about her condition and was making herself sicker in the process. As we conversed, I suddenly noticed that she was sitting still; she was no longer squirming. She had changed right before my eyes. It was amazing evidence of how much our spirit affects our body as well as our soul. This girl's spiritual reorientation gave her the hope and heart and direction to seek medical help. As she sought the Lord's guidance to get medical help for her condition, he answered her need, and in the process she began to learn how to enjoy life in the Lord who loves her. She learned to trust the Lord instead of blaming him for her problems—and what a difference it made!

Man is designed to have his life revolve around God, reigning in the *spirit* of man. The *Spirit of God* reigning in the *spirit of man* is what we would call the normal Christian life. That is the way man is designed to function, like a wheel rotating about its geometric center. But man in his natural, fallen state is like a wheel rotating off-center—eccentric. And even Christians who are not allowing Christ to reign as their Lord are displaying the same kind of imbalance. See Diagram B. The unregenerate man's life runs this way all the time and so does the Christian's, when he is operating in the flesh.

### The Division of Soul and Spirit

I have already mentioned that although there *is* a difference between soul and spirit, the distinction is not an easy one to make. We may come closer to understanding the difference, however, if we think of an animal—a dog, for instance—which certainly has a soul. The soul, remember, is composed of mind, emotions, and will, and a dog clearly *thinks, feels,* and *makes choices.* If you are his master, he shows emotion when you come home by wagging his tail. If you are a stranger trying to invade his household, he shows emotion very clearly in another way: by growling and showing his teeth. And it's not hard to see that dogs can think; they even cock their heads when they are puzzled. And when you try to get a dog to do what he doesn't want to do, you soon discover that he has a will.

On the other hand, although you can teach a dog to put his head on his paws and assume an attitude of prayer, you know he is not praying. He is just play-acting, for he has no spirit:

he doesn't worship God. Animals have self-conscious faculties of mind, emotion, and will, but they have no place for God in their lives. The spiritual quality of being able to relate to God is what makes man unique in all of creation. Man is designed to be *the dwelling place of God,* and for that reason he is a unique kind of creature. He is not just an animal, and he is not designed to be operating only on a *soul* level.

The point of all this is that we must seek to help people toward healing in the area in which the problem originates, keeping clearly in mind that the spiritual part of man is central to his being and thus pervades the whole man. Spiritual well-being promotes psychological and bodily health and can even help to override problems stemming from physical or psychological causes.

## The Gifts of Healing

In the listing of spiritual gifts found in 1 Corinthians there are two occurrences of the phrase "gifts of healings." Note that both "gifts" and "healings" are plural, not singular. We could take this to mean a multiplicity of healings, but I think it's much more reasonable to interpret this phrase as meaning there are different *kinds* of healing and the corresponding gifts to go with them. This would be consistent with the three-part nature of man, as we observe the healings taking place in men's bodies, souls, and spirits. Since spiritual gifts are given for the common good, to build up the body of Christ, I believe that God intends to employ the gifts of healing in the church, but only in accord with the whole body of revealed truth. Let me explain.

The saving work of Jesus Christ is designed to regenerate our spirits and save our souls; so I believe that spiritual well-being and psychological stability are the heritage of every Christian, subject to delivery on demand, as we walk by faith. That is, spiritual and emotional prosperity are meant to be ours through our risen Lord, as we draw on the resources available to us through his indwelling presence. I was impressed with this in reading Paul's prayer in Ephesians. Paul prays:

> . . . that you should know:
> - what is the hope of his calling,
> - what are the riches of his inheritance in the saints,
> - and what is the extremely "far out" greatness of his power toward us who believe, according to the energizing of the might of his strength—that power which he put to work in raising Christ from the dead and seating him . . . far above all authority . . . (Eph. 1:18–21, freely translated).

Paul exhausts his Greek vocabulary, using all the words he can muster to describe the liberating power God is exercising in our behalf—ending with an illustration: This is the kind of power which takes a dead man and makes him alive to rule over all! This is God's provision for our spiritual victory and emotional stability, available to us as we walk by faith.

**Unredeemed Bodies**

But in the physical realm, we have a different story. It's clear from the Scriptures that the redemption of our bodies is still in the future:

> We know that the whole creation has been groaning in travail together until now; and not only the creation, but we ourselves, who have the first fruits of the Spirit, groan inwardly as we wait for adoption as sons [literally *son-placing*: coming into the full possession of our inheritance in Christ], the redemption of our bodies (Rom. 8:22–23).

So our bodies are yet unredeemed, although they are *potentially* redeemed. The price has been paid in full for our total liberation, but we have yet to experience the total liberation of our bodies. That liberation is described in these terms, as still in the future: ". . . our commonwealth is in heaven, and from it we await a Savior, the Lord Jesus Christ, who will change our lowly body to be like his glorious body . . . (Phil. 3:20–21).

## Ultimate Healing

Make no mistake—I have no doubt about God's *ability* to heal the human body (after all, he made it, with all its intricacies), but he has not made himself *obliged* to heal our bodies, short of that day when we will experience the *redemption* of our bodies.

All the emphasis we see on physical healing today seems to me to ignore the fact that the ultimate healing for the Christian is to die! Any other kind of healing (whether real or fancied) is only a holding operation, postponing, but not forestalling the ultimate. For the non-Christian, it makes some sense to grasp frantically at every straw to sustain physical life. But for the Christian this kind of scrambling seems to be a lack either of understanding or confidence in what God has said on the subject.

Perhaps you are thinking: "Sure, that's easy to say when you're healthy. I'll bet Bob doesn't know what it's like to face the reality of physical pain and sickness." A few years ago you would have been right about me, but through two recent hospital episodes I have experienced the transcendent glory of the spiritual over the physical. I've learned, in the process, that the Lord is Lord of the coronary department as well as every other area of life. He can sustain us even when our hearts are failing!

In this area of physical healing I want to be an utter realist—in accord with the realistic truth of God. And I see plenty of evidence in the Bible that though God *can* heal, it doesn't always suit his sovereign purposes to do so. We have the instances of Paul's illness (Gal. 4:15), that of Trophimus

(2 Tim. 4:20), and of Timothy (1 Tim. 5:23), in which it is clear that the Lord was not obliged to supply physical healing but chose rather to use these physical infirmities to achieve his own sovereign purposes.

The gifts of healing, then, are to be employed in the context of these conclusions:

- Healing in the spirit and soul of man is inherent in and available through the finished work of our risen Lord. Victory is *promised* in these realms.

- Physical healing is *not* available on demand, but is subject to the sovereign will of God in the fulfilling of his good purposes.

- Ultimate physical healing *is promised* to every Christian when we receive our resurrection bodies, at our departure to be with Christ, whether at death or through the Rapture (1 Cor. 15:51–52).

Understanding of these facts can be vital in counseling. When the facts about healing, as set forth in Scripture, are clearly understood, much suffering can be relieved simply because confusion and false expectations have been removed. False hopes, being based on something untrue, always yield disappointment, while hope based on truth "does not disappoint us, because God's love has been poured into our hearts through the Holy Spirit which has been given to us" (Rom. 5:5).

# CHAPTER ELEVEN

# Moving toward Mental Health

Recently I heard a Christian psychiatrist friend of mine answer a question that stimulated my thinking regarding mental health. While he was teaching in a counselor's workshop, somebody asked him, "What is mental health?" In giving an answer, my friend gave me the impression that in psychology mental health was a rather nebulous term. It was interesting to me that such a widely used phrase seemed to defy definition, so I began to ponder the question for myself —what *is* mental health? And beyond merely defining the term, how do we learn to enjoy at least a relative degree of good mental health? Then it occurred to me that the Lord Jesus, in his earthly life and ministry, is a picture of perfect mental health. This thought triggered a series of questions relating to our own situation. For a complete list of these questions, in the form of a self-evaluation, look at Appendix E: "How Is Your Mental Health?"

## Tough Questions

Here are some of the tough questions I had to ask myself—and which I pose to you. First, "How well can you handle rejection?" Most of us have *plenty* of trouble handling feelings of rejection, thereby showing an impairment of mental health. And the next one, which is related to the first, is, "How does your love hold up in the face of rebuff?" Don't answer that yet—just think about it.

When I first put down these questions, it was just for my own information. But then I decided to try them out on somebody else, and my first victim was my wife. Her response was really funny. As she worked through the list in the living room, I was in the next room listening to her reactions. I chuckled as I heard her mumbling to herself with answers like this: "I'm learning" . . . "Forget it!" . . . "Lousy!" . . . "Pretty good" . . . "None of your business!"

After she got through, she came into the room where I was and said, "You're sadistic!"

But do you see the beauty of this response? She went through the whole list—a really tough list, and she wasn't threatened or put down. She showed a good degree of mental health. She had the liberty and understanding to realize that she was learning and growing in her ability to handle the difficult, trying things of life through the Lord.

Recently I laid the test on a group of pastors at a seminar and received similar reactions. Yet, in spite of its difficulty—for all of us—I think it's a valid subject to explore, one that can make us all more fulfilled and mentally healthy. Let's look at a few of the other questions:

How panic-proof are you in the face of pressure?
Are you at rest in the midst of a world in turmoil?
Are you able to relate objectively to the needs of others?
Do you generally have a good sense of personal worth?
How realistic is your assessment of your own importance?

They're pretty penetrating questions, aren't they?

One other question in particular—"How free are you from indulging in emotional thinking?"—makes me think of a girl who came into my office and said, "I want to talk to you about something because I really need an objective view." So we went over the matter together, and I gave her an objective appraisal to which she reacted quite emotionally. As she calmed down a bit, I said, "It looks to me as if you're indulging in a bit of subjective, emotional thinking." And she replied with considerable feeling, "I'm *not* emotional!" As soon as she said this, she got the point through her own emotional response, and as we laughed together over her subjective reaction, she began to take a more objective view.

## The Picture of Health

Now let's look at our model of mental health a little more closely and see what it can mean to our own well-being. As I stated earlier, *the Lord Jesus Christ is the picture of perfect mental health.* If you think through his earthly life and ministry, I think you'll agree with me. He was perfectly poised, loving, unhurried, non-defensive, and objectively at ease in every situation. He showed total emotional stability in the face of pressures the like of which you and I will never have to face. We see a *little* pressure—he got the works! "But," you might respond, "so what if the Lord Jesus epitomizes the absolute in emotional well-being and perfect mental health. What has that to do with anything? *He* has it, but how about us?" I'd like to pursue that and see how the fact that this is true of him really *can* make a difference to us.

## Handling Rejection

Let's go through some of these questions again and see how they apply to our Lord. The first one is: "How well can you take rejection?" Think through how the Lord Jesus took rejection. Isaiah writes of him that "he was despised and rejected by men; a man of sorrows . . ." (Isa. 53:3). Psalms 22:1 and Matthew 27:46 record his agonized cry from the cross, "My God, my God, why hast thou forsaken me?" He suffered absolute and utter rejection, including the rejection of his heavenly Father. He was truly God-forsaken in order that we may *never* have to be. Yet, it says that he "trusted to him who judges justly" (1 Pet. 2:23). Do you see what this is saying? He handled rejection *perfectly* by faith.

He handled rejection such as you and I will *never* have to face, *by faith*. He trusted in the One who had seemingly deserted him.

## Love That Doesn't Turn Off

Next question: "How does your love hold up in the face of rebuff?" Thinking of this, I was reminded of the Lord on the cross when they were driving the nails through his hands and his feet. What did he say? "Father, forgive them, for they know not what they do" (Luke 23:34). That's poise in the most dismal of circumstances. If you should try pounding nails through my hands and feet, I'm afraid I wouldn't react *quite* that way. I don't think any of us would, naturally. But the Lord Jesus handled it perfectly. He had perfect mental health, perfect emotional stability.

## Know Where You're Going?

Look at another question: "Do you have a clear sense of direction in a confused world?" In checking our Lord's life in regard to this, we need to look at a passage from the Gospel of John:

> The disciples said to him, "Rabbi, the Jews were but now seeking to stone you, and are you going there again?" Jesus answered, "Are there not twelve hours in the day? *If any one walks in the day, he does not stumble, because he sees the light of this world. But if any one walks in the night, he stumbles, because the light is not in him*" (John 11:8–10, italics mine).

On this occasion, Jesus was going to raise Lazarus from the dead. And what the Lord was saying is: "Really, I know what I'm doing; there's no problem in going back into Judea, even though I *was* threatened." You see, he had a perfect sense of timing and security in the midst of threatening circumstances because he had clear directions from his heavenly

Father. His purpose was to go where he was needed, even in the face of danger, to raise Lazarus from the dead—and thereby demonstrate who he was. He said, "I am the resurrection and the life . . ." (John 11:25). For him there was no problem; in a situation where his disciples demonstrated they were part of the confused world, Jesus had a clear sense of direction. In our human frailty you and I identify with his disciples, but in Christ we can identify with *him* and maintain our poise.

## Value Systems

Here's another question: "How fulfilling is your value system?" That's a deeply significant and far-reaching probe—one well worth thinking through. Many of the value systems men have adopted are totally unfulfilling. But if there's one thing I've learned about the Lord, it's that he wants us to be totally fulfilled people. He really cares that we have it all. He loves us so much that he doesn't want us to miss out on any good thing—that's the way he's disposed toward us. So we need to look at his value system and check *ours* against *his*.

## Winning by Losing

Jesus expressed his value system this way: "Truly, truly, I say to you, unless a grain of wheat falls into the earth and dies, it remains alone; but if it dies, it bears much fruit. He who loves his life loses it, and he who hates his life in this world will keep it for eternal life" (John 12:24–25).

Do you see what he's saying? He uses as an illustration a little grain of wheat, and says, *unless it falls into the ground and dies, it remains alone*. But, he says, *if it dies, it bears much fruit*. Then he follows with the application to us: *He who loves his life loses it, but he who hates his life in this world will keep it for eternal life*. In other words, if I seek to gratify my own self-centered desires, I'm going to lose out

because that's not the way things are in God's program. The world's value system is quite the opposite from our Lord's; it says "grab all you can, with both hands!" There's an enemy who has distorted man's thinking so that the world's value systems are all twisted.

The Lord Jesus wants us to get our values straight. He proved that he had his straight, because essentially he was talking about his own dying and bringing forth much fruit. And I'm part of that fruit; I have eternal life through his dying for me. Through most of my earlier years I was either atheistic or agnostic—God was nowhere in my program. But his love, expressed in the cross, got to me; nothing else would have reached my indifferent heart. When I really began to understand this principle of dying in order to live, employed by the Lord himself in the cross, I couldn't fight that. Love is the hardest thing in the world to fight. You don't fight it—you *join* it!

But the point is this: The Lord's value system was perfect. He not only told us that we were to fling away our lives and not to hang on like the world does, but he also showed us the way—by giving his life for us. The Scripture records of him, "Therefore God has highly exalted him . . ." (Phil. 2:9).

He says that if we're willing to lay our life on the line, then we will *gain* it. He is speaking here in spiritual terms, of our being self-giving instead of self-seeking. The one who hates his life in this world will keep it for eternal life. When he says, "He who hates his life in this world," we need to understand what he means by this. He's not saying we're to hate our life as related to the *created* world, for his creation is wholly to be admired and enjoyed. Rather, he is speaking of the world *system,* which has things so badly mangled by its fogged-up thinking. We are surely free to love the created world. I live in a forest setting, and I never get over its beauty. Our Lord knows we're not to hate this world; he wants us to be thankful for all he's put before us—the beauty and blessing of his own provision for us. But we *are* to hate worldly philosophies and thought patterns which are in opposition to him.

What does the Lord Jesus mean by hating one's life, though? That's the real issue at stake. As I see it, it all revolves around the illustration of the grain of wheat. In the case of that little kernel, it had to pour out the life it contained in order to bring forth multiplied life. In our case, as men and women, it involves considering our own plans and ambitions for worldly success and approval in low regard for the sake of others' good. Essentially, it means dying that others may live, just as with the grain of wheat. And the result for us and others is eternal, abundant life. It's the interesting paradox of winning by losing, of gaining by giving, of victory through surrender.

Also, we need to understand that *eternal life* in the Bible is literally "the life of the ages." It's unending because it is God's life, and it isn't just the life that we look forward to in eternity—it's life that is to begin *here and now.* I *have* eternal life now because the Lord has given it to me. I have it because he lives in me and he is eternal. He'll never end, and I'll never end because he lives in me. But the key thing about this life, the life of the ages, is that it is a new quality of life—it's not just endless quantity. For some, an endless quantity of the "status quo" would be an eternal hell, wouldn't it? Our Lord is talking about a renewed quality of life—that abundant life he has promised to his own.

**I Want My Rights!**

Let's consider one last question: "How willing are you to forego your rights?" When I think of this proposition, an old familiar story comes to mind. There was a dispute among the leadership in a church in which one of the leaders pounded the table and said, "I demand my rights!" One of his Christian brothers quietly replied, "Friend, if you had your rights, you'd be in hell!" He's right, and it's true of all of us. Again,

"How willing are you to forego your rights?" There's a current line of teaching which says that Christians don't have any rights, but that's not so—it's easy to prove scripturally. In 1 Corinthians 9, Paul talks about his rights. So we *do* have rights. But our highest right or privilege is to be willing to *forego* the exercise of our rights. Why? Because that's what our Lord did. This is pictured for us in Philippians:

> Have this mind among yourselves, which you have in Christ Jesus, who, though he was in the form of God, did not count equality with God a thing to be grasped, but emptied himself, taking the form of a servant, being born in the likeness of men. And being found in human form he humbled himself and became obedient unto death, even death on a cross (Phil. 2:5–8).

Here we see our Lord actually setting aside by his own volition his right to exercise the prerogatives of his deity. He willingly stepped down from heaven to earth into the human family and entered history as a baby in a cave made to shelter animals—from heaven's glory to a grubby little manger. I always like to remember that it was a dirty stable—there was undoubtedly manure on the floor. It wasn't like the pictures on our Christmas cards. Into this humble scene stepped the Lord of glory, foregoing his rights. He could have stayed in heaven and said, "All that miserable lot down there—that bunch of rebels—can go to hell." And he would have been perfectly righteous in doing it. (I don't know if you believe that, but I do. It's true, because we're a rebel race at heart, and God owes salvation to *none* of us.)

But he didn't do that. He said, "All those rebels are dear to me; they need me. They need the expression of love that only I can give. They need a Savior. If it means I must move into that earthly vale of tears and forego my rights, I'll do it!" So he came, the sinless Son of God, and was made sin for us that we might be reconciled to God through him: "God was in Christ reconciling the world to himself, not counting their trespasses against them . . ." (2 Cor. 5:19). This is the central fact of unqualified love that never changes. Who doesn't want that kind of love? It became available to us because Christ was willing to set aside the exercise of his rights.

## Peace with God

In the setting aside of his rights to die for us, Jesus accomplished an otherwise impossible feat: our justification before God. The Webster Dictionary definition of justification is most revealing: *to be justified is to be declared blameless of sin on the ground of Christ's righteousness,* imputed by faith. Webster knew his theology, it appears. If there is anything that all of us want (in our right mind at least), it is to be declared blameless of sin. It isn't that we haven't sinned —we have, and we frankly acknowledge it, I trust. But what we all need is some way of dealing with it. That's what God has given us in the reconciling work of his Son, making us right with God. This is the essential good news of the gospel: that God has made perfect provision for us, from our estranged state, to enter back into a love relationship with him. What he is really saying is this: "I'm not fighting you, now why don't you stop fighting me?"

*That's the beginning of mental health*—to have peace between you and God. As long as you're fighting the one who made you, you'll never be in anything but turmoil. You begin to enter into mental health by saying, "Thanks, Lord, for making perfect provision in the cross to put away my sins." And in that same text in 2 Corinthians it says there's only one action needed on your part: "We beseech you on behalf of Christ, be reconciled to God" (2 Cor. 5:20). God doesn't hold back—if there's any holding back, it is *on our part.* Our emotional well-being and good mental health start when we stop holding back and submit willingly to the lordship of Jesus Christ. That's what will bring peace of heart and freedom from guilt to those we counsel. Not only that, but he offers his loving presence and guidance to those who acknowledge his Lordship. Our mental health is directly proportional to how well we're relating to the resources available to us in Jesus Christ.

### Available on Demand

And to those who know Him, good mental health is available, on demand, by faith. It is a matter of simply responding to the Lord in the way that he's made available to us. ". . . we have this treasure in earthen vessels, that the excellency of the power may be seen to be of God and not of us" (2 Cor. 4:7, KJV). A beautiful figure—an earthen vessel—that's just an old clay pot, you know. It is usually slightly cracked, yet it contains a tremendous treasure—the Lord Jesus himself. Christian life is enjoying the fact that a very flawed vessel contains a wonderfully beautiful and attractive treasure—the Lord himself. If we understand this, there is no more need to "fake it," no big "cover up" is necessary. We can just be ourselves in Christ. What a relief! Then we are simply in our right minds, responding to our indwelling Lord, thus becoming display cases for the great treasure that the Lord has invested in us—himself!

In ourselves, we're wholly inadequate—perfectly equipped to do absolutely nothing that's worthwhile and permanent. But the Lord says, "You're right, I know you're inadequate, but you have me, don't you?" And on that basis, we can handle anything that comes. That's fabulous truth, and it's the basis of mental health.

### Achieving Wholeness—A Process

You can find out how well you're responding to his life by reviewing the remaining questions on the self-evaluation in Appendix E. It's just for your information—it's a personal inventory. You don't have to share it with anybody. And you need not feel threatened by it, for the Lord Jesus is available to give you perfect mental health. But whether you choose to review the questions or not, you can begin to relate more closely to the adequacy of the risen Lord Jesus who lives in you (I trust) and thus enjoy mental health. Then you can share the wealth of this great treasure with those whom you are trying to help.

Just think through these questions in terms of how we are to relate to the Lord Jesus. If you're like everybody else, you'll say, "I'm not doing so hot, but I'm growing. I'm learning." And that's where everybody is. Nobody has arrived at perfection, as I'm sure you're aware. We're all men and women under construction. But thank God for a *great* Building Contractor (a former carpenter) who knows his business.

The process is described as follows: ". . . present your bodies as a living sacrifice, holy and acceptable to God, which is your spiritual worship. Do not be conformed to this world but be transformed by the *renewal of your mind* . . ." (Rom. 12:1*b*, 2, italics mine).

As we allow the Lord Jesus to be constantly renewing our mind, we are enjoying good mental health.

# CHAPTER TWELVE

# Healing Hurting Hearts

Several issues demand the loving attention of Christian counselors more than others. Among these are *forgiveness, deliverance* from sin's power, the *lordship* and *love* of Christ. And though we've treated the matter of deliverance earlier, in chapter 8, perhaps it would not be amiss to see the issues of forgiveness and deliverance side by side in a brief discussion of the redemptive truth applying to each. Then we can profitably consider the value of the lordship and love of our Lord Jesus in added perspective. These are major issues in our move toward healing hurting hearts.

## Our Need of Forgiveness

The first of these levels of freedom concerns our need for forgiveness. The problem of guilt is far deeper and more pervasive than we generally understand. Occasionally, this need for forgiveness shows up in newspaper accounts of criminals who turn themselves in even after they have escaped detection. The only explanation for such action is their need to purge their conscience of an unbearable sense of guilt. All of us, criminals or not, have felt the inner pangs of guilt produced by wrong actions and attitudes. If you doubt the reality of this, try reading through our Lord's words in the Sermon on the Mount (Matthew 5 through 7). These words of our Lord were designed to accentuate our sense of guilt.

All of us have a deep need for forgiveness and the freedom from guilt it provides. The Scripture is clear that we do not have to be guilt-ridden people, so for our own sake and for those we have opportunity to counsel, we must constantly appropriate the means God has made available to us for forgiveness. Applying the truth of 1 John 1, is a direct answer to this universal need. John tells us that we're kidding ourselves and calling God a liar if we say we have no sin or have not sinned (1 John 1:8, 10). But if we simply admit our sin to God, he promises to forgive us and cleanse us from all unrighteousness: "If we confess our sins, he [God] is faithful and just, and will forgive our sins and cleanse us from all unrighteousness" (1 John 1:9). The ground of this forgiveness is the cross of Christ, for "the blood of Jesus Christ his Son cleanses us from all sin" (1 John 1:7).

Diagram C helps us to visualize God's *Forgiveness Cycle*—a procedure we need to employ consistently to put down any possibility of carrying around a load of guilt. Note that our problem starts with *temptation* (at the top of the circle), a solicitation to sin. Temptation is *not sin,* for you will recall of our Lord Jesus that he "in every respect has been *tempted* as we are, yet *without sinning*" (Heb. 4:15*b*, italics mine). But succumbing to temptation becomes *sin,* which must then somehow be put away, since it hinders our fellowship with God.

The next step is *repentance,* which is "a change of mind." Repentance is a good word, though we often try to avoid it. It is not just being sorry we were caught, but rather it involves a thoroughgoing change of mental attitude about the act of sin which has been committed. The word *repentance* is not in this text, but it is implicit as the prelude to *confession,* for to confess means "to say the same thing" about my sin as God says about it. Since my mind somehow justified the act, leading to its commission, I must have a change of mind in order to acknowledge that God was right all along. So I confess my sin: not just by saying to God, "I confess my sin," but by tell-

*DIAGRAM C*

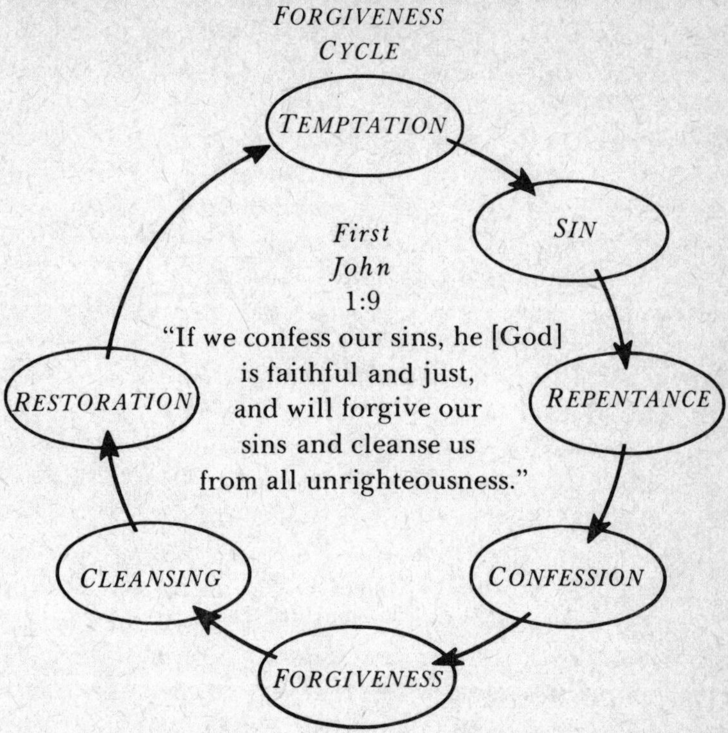

*FORGIVENESS CYCLE*

*TEMPTATION*

*SIN*

*REPENTANCE*

*CONFESSION*

*FORGIVENESS*

*CLEANSING*

*RESTORATION*

*First John* 1:9
"If we confess our sins, he [God] is faithful and just, and will forgive our sins and cleanse us from all unrighteousness."

ing him specifically what I did wrong and agreeing with him that it *was* wrong. On that basis he supplies complete and total *forgiveness* and *cleansing*. Forgiveness is for my sake—to free me from guilt, while cleansing is to fit me once again for fellowship with a holy God. And note—it's cleansing *from all unrighteousness*. There is no exclusion: No sin can possibly be bad enough to permanently disrupt my fellowship with God. The only condition God stipulates is my freely acknowledging my sin in confession. Restoration into the full enjoyment of my life and fellowship with the Lord is the result. From there we go back to the top of the cycle and face the next temptation. How we all need this blessed provision!

*DIAGRAM D*

*DELIVERANCE CYCLE*

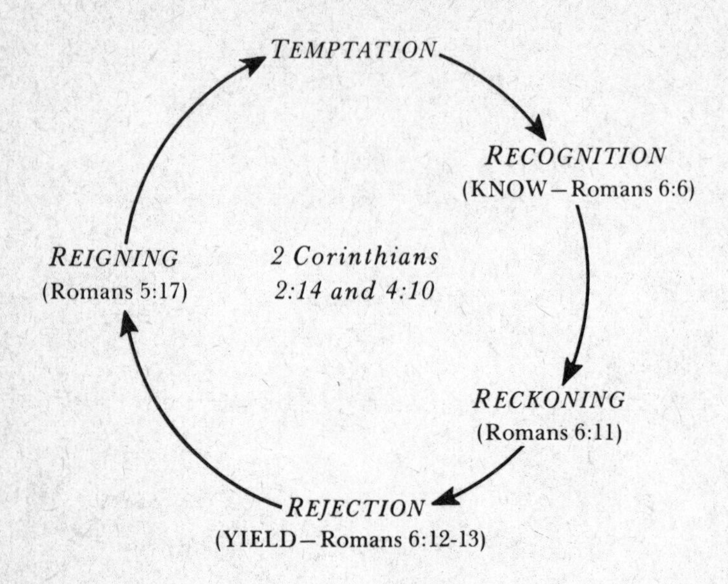


**Power to Deliver**

As good and necessary as this cycle is, better still is the *Deliverance Cycle*. Forgiveness deals with the problem of guilt, but our even deeper need is to be delivered from the power of sin. God knows this and has made perfect provision for setting us free from sin's domination. He says, ". . . sin will have no dominion over you, since you are not under law but under grace" (Rom. 6:14). I often think how basically unavailing are man's solutions as compared with God's. We pardon a criminal and turn him loose to perpetrate the same crimes. God knows better than that. He pardons our sin, then changes us from the inside out to free us from sin's power. The gospel of Christ includes both *forgiveness* and *deliverance.*

Note that the *Deliverance Cycle* in Diagram D starts with

the same problem, *temptation,* but instead of moving to *sin,* the next step in the cycle is *recognition.* Recognition is twofold: there is recognition of (1) the solicitation to sin and (2) freedom in Christ *not* to sin. For we know that "our old man was put to death with Christ in order that . . . we may no longer be enslaved to sin" (Rom. 6:6). Knowing this fact, we can then move to *reckoning* it as true by faith. That is, we simply believe what God has said about our liberation from sin's enslaving power. On this basis we can move to the *rejection* of the call to sin by yielding ourselves to God rather than to sin's power (Rom. 6:12–13). The result: We can go on *reigning* in life through Jesus Christ (Rom. 5:17*b*), which is to "live like a king" instead of like a slave. What a great truth to share with those who wear the heavy shackles of sin's slavery! It is the Lordship and love of Jesus Christ that makes all this possible. He has conquered through love and is now reigning in love.

**Lordship and Love**

Sometimes we Christians tend to think we have a tough time of it, and in some ways we do. We face a hostile world. The world isn't friendly to us; the Lord told us it wouldn't be. And we face an implacable enemy who is very powerful and intensely active these days. That old accuser, Satan, seems to take fiendish delight in making Christians miserable. So we really do face staggering opposition. Considering the situation, we could take a "poor me" attitude, but we need not and *should* not because in our Lord Jesus we have one who is greater than the world and Satan.

It helps me keep things in perspective to look back at the first century of Christian life. The background of Paul's word to the Corinthians helps us to understand that we really don't have it so bad. Hear what Paul writes: "Therefore I want you to understand that no one speaking by the Spirit of God ever says 'Jesus be cursed!' and no one can say

'Jesus is Lord' except by the Holy Spirit" (1 Cor. 12:3). This statement seems to be somewhat extraneous to its context, but if we understand something of the historical background, it begins to fit. If you had been a Christian in the first century, you might quite possibly have been haled before a Roman magistrate for treason. It was treason not to worship the Emperor, Caesar, as god. He was in their pantheon of gods, and you were supposed to say "Caesar is lord!" And in this courtroom scene the magistrate might have said to you, "Well, Octavius (or whatever your name is), this is really a simple matter. All you have to do is say before this court, 'Jesus be damned; Caesar is lord!' and we will let you go." But there were many Christians who died in the arena, or on a cross, or as a flaming torch, because they insisted "*Jesus* is Lord!," refusing to say "Caesar is lord." That is why this statement of the apostle's is so significant. As you can see, there was a great deal at stake. It was no light matter to say "Jesus is Lord!" in those days. The reason Paul adds, "No one can say 'Jesus is Lord' except by the Holy Spirit," is that it took the strengthening, enabling ministry of the strong Spirit of God to give God's people the courage to stand on the truth that Jesus is Lord.

Recently I read a very interesting book by Col. Robinson Risner. If I remember correctly, he was the first Vietnam POW to step out of the plane at Clark Air Force Base in the Philippines to address us on national television. His book is entitled, *The Passing of the Night*. That's a very apt title, for it was quite a night, believe me, that he endured. The book is a description of the awful, gruesome experience he had for seven and one-half years as a prisoner of war in a North Vietnamese prison. It is not exactly pleasant reading; in fact, it is a very sobering book. But I wanted to read it because I have a friend who had stayed at the "Hanoi Hilton," as they called it, for five and a half years, and I wanted to understand something of how he would feel and think as a result of his experience.

All through the book I could only marvel at the integrity and stability of Robbie Risner as he faced unbelievable stress and torture. Then I found the explanation: You guessed it—he's a Christian. He kept insisting that Jesus is Lord in the midst of that very hostile and terrifying situation. I got some of the inside information on Robbie's story through contacts of my POW friend. I learned that my friend said to his liaison officer (who happened, by God's appointment, to be a Christian man), "This man Robbie has something I don't understand, something I don't know anything about. Will you tell me about it?" You can imagine what a great time that Christian officer had in explaining to him that Robbie's integrity was an expression of the authority of faith in Jesus Christ, because Robbie had really committed himself to the lordship of Christ in his life. When everything looked bleak, he was still able to say in his heart—and by his life—"Jesus is Lord!" This is an instance of the application of that truth in one man's life just as the passage from Corinthians highlights the same truth in the lives of those early Christians.

What is the secret of spiritual strength and stability? The explanation is in two words: LORDSHIP and LOVE. I have found that it's remarkable what happens when we learn to say "Jesus is Lord!" in any situation—and it is the same, whether in the first or the twentieth century. It makes no difference whether it is in a prison or a pew, and it applies equally well to individuals as it does to groups of individuals like a local church. Where Jesus is Lord, there is liberty, prosperity, strength, stability—all the good things you and I really long for and love to enjoy.

In Acts 10:36 the Apostle Peter, speaking in the home of a Roman soldier, made an interesting statement on this subject. He was telling Cornelius and his friend the gospel. Speaking of the Lord Jesus, he said, "You know the word which he [God] sent to Israel, preaching good news of peace by Jesus Christ . . ." and he adds, as a parenthetical thought, ". . . he is Lord of all . . ." Here he gives us the key to

Christian life: *"He is Lord of all."* Some parenthesis, I'd say! Let's look at two details in this statement: First, what is meant by lordship, and second, what is included in that "all" in "he is Lord of *all.*" In the monumental *Theological Dictionary of the New Testament* edited by Kittel and Friedrich, there is an extensive treatment of this word "Lord." The following definition is gleaned from the study of lordship included there:

**Lordship Means Authority**

Essentially, this word "Lord" applies to *one who has ultimate, decisive authority*. It also speaks of *one who is strong, competent, important, and powerful,* thus *able to rule.* Lordship *also denotes possession,* that is, *having the legal right of ownership* and the *final word on the disposition of that which he owns.* It also has the sense of priority. "Lord" is equivalent to the "Chief," or the "Boss," the one on top—the one who is in charge.

Now if you take all these aspects of the meaning of the word "Lord" and apply them to the Lord Jesus, in summary you find we can say of him that he is the source of power and authority. His own words say it—those amazing words given to encourage his disciples: "All authority in heaven and on earth has been given to me" (Matt. 28:18). That sounds like quite enough power, doesn't it? He has all there is. He's the strong one, fully competent. Then he adds these wonderful words (which I paraphrase), *"And I'm with you"* (Matt. 28:20*b*). The fact that he has all power might just scare us, but when he says, "I'm with you," he makes a commitment to use that power on our behalf. It's clear why he said this to his disciples as they faced the humanly impossible task of going out and reaching the world with the gospel. Eleven weaklings were all Jesus had to work with—so they needed to hear, "All power is given to me, and I'm with you." That's his Lordship being declared to men who *had* to know their resources.

Also, the Lord Jesus is the one (since he made us) who knows the score; that is, he knows what's going on; he has all the information about our specific situation and need. Paul says of him, "In him are hid all the treasures of wisdom and knowledge" (Col. 2:3). And as Lord, he is also *the final evaluator* of all of us. I think sometimes we Christians think that because salvation is by grace, the Lord is never going to evaluate our works. But the Bible does not tell us that. It says that "we must all appear before the judgment seat of Christ" (2 Cor. 5:10) to see how we've done. This is to be an evaluation, not a judgment to condemnation. The Lord, as Lord, has the right to evaluate what has been going on in us. There is something at stake in the Christian life. He has something for us to do, and we are held accountable to do what he says. So his Lordship gives him this right of final evaluation.

Then, he is the one who owns everything—that is also implicit in this word "Lord." And because he owns everything, he has the right to rule, having full authority over that which is his. The words "You are not your own; you were bought with a price" (1 Cor. 6:19*b*) express that truth. He says, "I own you on two counts: I made you, and I redeemed you." By creation and redemption, he owns us; we are his.

## Lord of Creation and Re-Creation

Now let's turn and look at the "all" in Peter's words: "He is Lord of all." First, he is the Lord over *all creation*. Paul tells us in Colossians,

> . . . for in him all things were created, in heaven and on earth, visible and invisible, whether thrones or dominions or principalities or authorities—all things were created through him and for him. He is before all things, and in him all things hold together (Col. 1:16–17).

Did you notice the repetition of "all things" coupled with

every kind of preposition language affords? All things were created *by* him . . . *in* him . . . *through* him . . . and *for* him. He is *before* all things . . . and all things hold together *in* him. *He is Lord over all creation.*

Paul goes on to say he is Lord over the new creation—that's us, the church, his people: "He is the head of the body, the church; he is the beginning, the first-born from the dead, that in everything he might be preeminent (Col. 1:18). So his lordship is unmistakably over *all*. Yet the only ones who really respond to his lordship are those who are his. We are the ones who have acknowledged his lordship—if not always in particular, at least as a general principle. Toward us he has two very wonderful characteristics. He is called "the Lord of the harvest," and "the Lord of the sabbath." These are significant terms. "The Lord of the harvest" means that he is the one who puts his people to work where he wants them, doing what he wants them to do, and that he exercises his right to send forth his workers as he wills. "The Lord of the sabbath" means that he is able to give rest in the midst of an intensely active life. It's the rest of faith. This subject is treated in detail in the next chapter.

I like the fact that the Lord Jesus insists on being who he is. There's no way he can be anything else but *Lord*. I might be confused as to who he is, but he isn't; he always knows he is Lord. Looking back at my own Christian life, I recall quite clearly that I didn't really understand the lordship of Christ when I first came to him. I knew he was some kind of authoritative person, otherwise I wouldn't have committed my life to him. But I didn't understand that the name of the game was lordship. However, he was never confused. Soon after I came to Christ I found him insisting that I do things his way. "Sorry, Bob, you're a nice fellow and all that, but I'm not going to bend my standards for you; you've got to bend to me." And I have learned to say, "Yes, Lord, I get the picture." I began to learn that the process of growth in the

Christian life is an increasing understanding and willing acceptance of who he is: *Jesus is Lord.*

Jesus is Lord not only in the sense that he is immanent in the universe, but he also wants to be Lord, personally, in each of us. The lordship of Christ is the greatest truth I know because it opens the door to my becoming the man I really want to be! He is committed to the fulfillment of my Christian manhood, and he's not going to quit until he's got the job done, for which I'm tremendously thankful. More than that, he is the one who lives in me, having *all* the answers to *all* the problems in life. He will undertake the responsibility for my total well-being, but on one basis only: if I am willing to *give* him that responsibility. Very simply, I just need to say, consistently and repeatedly, as those others I have mentioned have said, "Jesus is Lord." In every problem I face I can say, "Lord, you really are Lord to me right now, for this situation." This is the word we need to share with those we are called to counsel.

In his *Theological Dictionary,* Gerhard Kittel makes what I think is an outstanding statement on this subject:

> [In the Lordship of Christ] firmly grasped, both in the emotions and will, the man [responding to his Lordship] receives unconditionally binding direction which gives meaning, measure, and purpose to his life; and which demands an obedience that is not exhausted in the cultivation of feeling, but manifests itself in concrete action.

In other words, the lordship of Christ in me means action, exciting action. Then he adds,

> Only when man is confronted with the God who made him, the One who is the absolute authority, before which it is freedom, rather than bondage, to bow, [is there any true liberation].

That's a great statement. Bondage is freedom—if it is bondage to Jesus Christ. Paul loved to call himself the "bond-slave" of Jesus Christ. This is willing slavery which means liberty. Paradoxical? Yes, but wonderfully true. And the reason this arrangement is so desirable is that in Christ we are confronted with one who woos our hearts with the authority of ministering and forgiving love. He doesn't come at us arbitrarily; he constantly appeals to us to move with him. Only in Christ do we see lordship manifested in all its attractive power and desirability.

## Our Response

Now, there is a problem, of course: it's *our performance*. Response to Christ's lordship is not perfect in any one of us. A dear friend of mine has been kind enough to take on the task of teaching me how to swing a golf club—no small job, believe me. I don't know if you've ever tried to learn to play golf, especially in your old age, but those who have know that the golf swing is very unnatural. Nevertheless, it's dead right. The body mechanics are undeniably true—*doing* it is another story. My friend was showing me the "weak position" of the right arm. Golf is essentially a left-handed game; the right arm is supposed to follow the action of the left side—not dominate it. At this point, he observed that the right arm is like the flesh, always trying to overpower the action. But when that happens, you have just lost your golf swing. If you keep the right arm out of the way (in the weak position), you may have a golf swing. But doing it is difficult, for in most of us the right arm is dominant. Similarly, the problem in experiencing the lordship of Christ is actually *doing* it. The old right arm of the flesh gets in there. "I can do it, Lord. I don't need you for this. I can do *some* things myself, can't I?" But the Lord says no; "Without me you can do nothing." Jesus is LORD of ALL.

Even so, he doesn't lord it over us. He always couples LORDSHIP with LOVE. He *could* just tell us what to do and make us do it, but he doesn't. He always exercises his right to rule *in love,* in gracious consideration of that love relationship he has with us. And on that basis, he always seeks our consent and asks us to cooperate with his program; he doesn't coerce us into reluctant obedience.

When I was in college, I had two dogs. One was a beautiful gold-colored collie with a white ruff named Jimmie, and the other was a magnificent silver-and-black longhaired German shepherd named Pat. They were quite an impressive pair, and everywhere they went with me they attracted attention. They were also a very interesting behavioral study. Jimmie, with all his beauty, was a pain because he had an obedience problem. He never wanted to do what I told him. If I finally insisted, and worked at it to make him behave, he'd do it, but it was always a struggle. Some of us are like that with the Lord, aren't we? But Pat was quite different. He was eager to please. Whenever I showed up, he was right there ready to go, looking at me with an expectant look, eager to do whatever I had in mind, and enjoying every moment of it. Jimmie wasn't enjoying it very much because he only obeyed under pressure; Pat was loving every moment of it.

For me those dogs were a graphic picture of two kinds of Christians, showing two kinds of response to the lordship of Christ. I want to be a "Pat," not a "Jimmie," in case you're in doubt. Can you imagine the Lord's delight in us if we approached all of life this way? "Here I am, Lord, ready to go. Whatever you have in mind for today, let's do it together." We could move in every situation, whether it's playing golf or facing into a problem with confident, eager expectation.

Lordship and love, love and lordship—a great combination. If there is anything designed to give us the liberty and fulness of life, I submit that these two are the combination of features that make for a *great life*.

In our counseling ministry we need to ask our counselees: Where are you in this program? That's what the Lord is always concerned about. Are you enjoying all he's made you to be? Have you discovered that he's given you a personality and a ministry, in addition to gifts, talents, and opportunities? He wants you to use all of them and *live* a little. Unfortunately there are many Christians who have heard a lot of truth but who are not really living joyfully. I think the reason is simple: They haven't learned yet how to take that "weak position." The right arm, the flesh, is trying to overpower the spiritual life. The flesh is too often in the ascendancy. Consequently, we're missing out on much of what the Lord has in mind for us.

**For VIP's**

I like to ask people the question, "Are you a VIP?" (that means, "Very Important Person"). You may ask, "A VIP in whose eyes? I'm important to somebody. My wife (or my husband) loves me. The kids don't think I'm too bad. I'm important to them. At least, I bring home the paycheck regularly." But I really mean: Do you think you are important in the eyes of the one who counts most—important in God's eyes? I submit to you that *you are. You're very important to him.* He's proved it to you. How? He's offered to be your Lord! He's made himself wholly available to you. Now reverse the arrows. *He* is also a very important person to *you* because he is Lord. No matter what anybody else will ever have to say about it, the Apostle Paul said the final word on this subject:

> Therefore God has highly exalted him and bestowed on him the name which is above every name, that at the name of Jesus every knee should bow, in heaven and on earth and under the earth, and every tongue confess that *Jesus Christ is Lord,* to the glory of God the Father (Phil. 2:9–11, italics mine).

The reason this double-edged truth is so very important is that many people sell themselves short, and thereby sell the

Lord short. So many say or think, "Poor little me. I don't have anything; I can't do anything; I'm not important." Not only is that not true, but such an attitude speaks very poorly for the Lord who loves you so much. You are *you*, and you need to understand and enjoy that sense of importance, that dignity of human personality which is the privilege of everyone of us who is indwelt by the Lord Jesus. What a joy—to tell those we are trying to help: Jesus is Lord! And he loves you!

# CHAPTER THIRTEEN

# Entering God's Rest

Having learned something of our own makeup and that of our enemies, we must now seek to understand the *mainline principle* God has given us as the major, positive operating feature of life: *how to rest while working.* This one principle is the key to an effective and fulfilled life and is applicable for both preventive and corrective maintenance. It is another way of describing our walk of faith.

Our approach may seem a bit strange and oblique, for it involves a study of a most unlikely subject—the sabbath. But as we proceed, I think you'll agree that God wants to teach us some vital truth through this rather obscure subject.

## What's the Sabbath All About?

There is a remarkable lack of basic understanding about the sabbath, perhaps not without good reason. For right in the midst of God's commandments covering the most significant and far-reaching moral and spiritual issues there is this almost capricious and seemingly irrelevant word:

> Remember the sabbath day, to keep it holy. Six days you shall labor, and do all your work; but the seventh day is a sabbath to the Lord your God; in it you shall not do any work, you, or your son, or your daughter, your manservant, or your maidservant, or your cattle, or the sojourner who is within your gates; for in six days the Lord made heaven and earth, the sea, and all

> that is in them, and rested the seventh day; therefore the Lord blessed the sabbath day and hallowed it (Ex. 20:8–11).

For such a seemingly inconsequential matter, the Lord speaks at considerable length on this subject, in contrast with "Thou shalt not kill" (Ex. 20:13) a few verses later. He has just four words to say about murder, but ninety-four words on the sabbath. How come? Is the sabbath really that important? Many of us don't pay the slightest attention to this fourth commandment in God's law.

So what's happened? Did God make a mistake? Is his Word less than inspired? What's wrong here?

I've learned that any apparent anomaly in the Word of God is a clue that shouts out loud for further investigation. And usually, further study reveals a most significant vein of truth. God likes to intrigue our thinking: "It is the glory of God to conceal things, but the glory of kings is to search things out" (Prov. 25:2). Let's be God's royal family.

I have several lengthy books in my library concerning the sabbath which completely miss the point, and there are sabbatarian sects that do likewise. Many have argued for lifetimes about which day to keep, thereby obscuring the real issue and missing the point of God's truth. The sabbath was a key issue with the Jews in our Lord's day, but neither then nor now does there seem to be much light generated as to its real significance. It seems that we tend either to overwork the subject in a legalistic nit-picking way or else to slide right by without trying to discover the real import of the sabbath.

**Facing Some Problems**

Perhaps the best way to begin our investigation of the sabbath and its significance is to confront some of the obvious problems about it and ask some crucial questions. Here are some rather intriguing and puzzling facts to consider:

1. *All except the sabbath commandment are repeated in the New Testament.* For instance, "Honor your father and your mother . . . " Exodus 20:12 is repeated in Ephesians 6:2. Also, "Do not lie to one another . . ." Colossians 3:9 is the equivalent of "You shall not bear false witness . . ." in Exodus 20:16.

2. *There is no equivalent to the sabbath commandment given in the New Testament.* On the contrary, in the New Testament we read: "One man esteems one day as better than another, while another man esteems all days alike. Let every one be fully convinced in his own mind" (Rom. 14:5).

3. *The Lord Jesus seemed to take particular pains to do some of his works on the sabbath day* (e.g. John 5:2–18).

It seems there's something wrong here, a glaring inconsistency between the testimonies of the Old and New Testaments. Let's try to unravel the puzzle by asking (and answering) some crucial questions: 1) What does "sabbath" mean? 2) To whom was the sabbath given? 3) What is God's *intent* in the sabbath idea? 4) Is there a New Testament parallel or fulfillment of the sabbath? If so—what is it?

In regard to the first question, I used to think that sabbath meant "seventh," since it was the seventh day, but now I know that *sabbath is from a Hebrew word which means "rest."* Keep that in mind, for its significance carries all the way through our study.

## Commanded–To Whom?

The sabbath was given as a command to the nation Israel and was invested by God with a "sign" character:

"Say to the people of Israel, 'You shall keep my sabbaths, for this is a *sign* between me and you throughout your generations, that you may know that I, the Lord, sanctify you. . . . Therefore the people of Israel shall keep the sabbath, observing the sabbath throughout their generations, as a perpetual covenant.

It is a *sign* for ever between me and the people of Israel . . .' " (Ex. 31:13 and 16–17, italics mine).

Therefore [for this reason] he says, the Lord commanded Israel to keep the sabbath. For *what* reason? It was to help them remember how the Lord redeemed them from slavery. After all, it should have seemed like a pretty good idea to them, since they had been seven-day-a-week slaves! The sabbath was to be a time of memorial and meditation on God's redemptive work of freeing the slaves.

The law, including the sabbath command, was *not* given to the Gentile nations: "When Gentiles *who have not the law* . . ." (Rom. 2:14, italics mine). Nor was the commandment given to Christians: "Therefore let no one pass judgment on you in questions of food and drink or with regard to a festival or a new moon or a sabbath" (Col. 2:16).

So what's it all about? Should we ignore the whole business unless we happen to be Jews? No. Let's not give up too soon. Remember (1) that we need to try to discover God's *intent* in the sabbath idea, and (2) that the nation Israel is designed to picture the individual Christian believer so that we may learn from Israel's history (1 Cor. 10:11).

**What's the Idea?**

In giving the sabbath command to Israel notice that the Lord relates it to the creation account in Genesis: ". . . for in six days the Lord made heaven and earth . . . and rested the seventh day; therefore the Lord blessed the sabbath day and hallowed it" (Ex. 20:11). Apparently God wanted his people to reflect back upon the rest God was enjoying following his creative activity as we read in the Genesis account: "So God blessed the seventh day . . . because on it God rested from all his work which he had done in creation" (Gen. 2:3).

But what is the nature of his rest? Was God tired? Did he

run out of energy? If we understand that God is the source of *all* power and energy, then it's clear that he was not suffering from an energy shortage. And according to Isaiah, he doesn't get tired, for "The Lord is the everlasting God, the Creator of the ends of the earth. He does not faint or grow weary . . ." (Isa. 40:28).

What, then, is the nature of this rest? Well, first it seems obvious that God had ceased from his activity, so inactivity is *part* of it. But I think there's more. When God had finished his work of creation, the account in Genesis says, "God saw everything that he had made, and behold, it was very good" (Gen. 1:31). The Lord was simply *enjoying* his creative handiwork, and this is the key ingredient in God's rest—his entering into and enjoying all that he had made. The first clue as to God's intent in the sabbath, then, is this picture of the God of creation relaxing and enjoying the result of his work.

## God Went Back to Work

This peaceful rest of God, however, was brought to an abrupt end. In the very next chapter of Genesis (Chapter 3) we read of the entrance of sin into the picture, and God had to start working again! Because of his great love, he could not rest *apart* from his creation (man), and he couldn't rest *in* man because he had turned away from God. His first work was the work of creation, but now he engages in the work of re-creation, the redemption of an alienated race of men to make them part of a *new* creation. The balance of the biblical record is the account of God's redemptive work to restore the *rest* that was lost through sin to both God and man. We see man's need for reentry into that rest in such Scriptures as these:

Therefore, while the promise of *entering his* [God's] *rest* remains, let us fear lest any of you be judged to have failed to reach it (Heb. 4:1, italics mine).

So then, *there remains a sabbath rest for the people of God;* for whoever *enters God's rest* also ceases from his labors as God did from his (Heb. 4:9–10, italics mine).

Let us therefore strive *to enter that rest* . . . (Heb. 4:11*a*, italics mine).

On God's side of the question, we see that the restoration of rest for him comes through the responsiveness of men's hearts in the obedience of faith. In Isaiah 66 we read: "Thus says the Lord: 'Heaven is my throne and the earth is my footstool; what is the house which you would build for me, and *what is the place of my rest?*' " (Isa. 66:1, italics mine). (Notice that the universe is just so much furniture to God!) Here the Lord asks the most pointed question of all time: Where do you think I should live, and where is the place I can call "home" and enjoy my rest? He answers his own question in the next verse: ". . . this is the man to whom I will look, he that is humble and contrite in spirit, and trembles at my word" (Isa. 66:2).

*For what* will God look to this man? Is it not for the place *where he can rest and feel at home?* And what makes it possible? Is it not the inward attitude of that man's heart? Humility—the opposite of pride; contrition of spirit—the opposite of hypocrisy and cover-up; trembling at God's word —the opposite of ignoring God or resisting him; these are the things which make God feel at home and at rest in the heart of man. The heart of the man who denies God entrance is the only place in the universe where *God is denied access.*

Hell is going to be an eternal pain in the heart of God because the ones who go there refused him a home. They resisted his offer to enjoy the life and presence of the One who made them and who has yearned to restore the rest they have missed. The ultimate expression of missing God's rest is hell, while the current evidence of men having missed God's rest is the restlessness of the age—men looking everywhere and trying everything (except God) to gain the satisfaction and fulfillment they lack. It's no wonder Christ pleads, "Behold, I stand at the door and knock . . ." (Rev. 3:20). He is saying, "Won't you let me in?"

**My Name Is Israel**

Returning to God's key example from which we are to learn, look at Israel's heart in response to God's appeal, recorded in his word to the Hebrews:

> Therefore, as the Holy Spirit says, "Today, when you hear his voice, do not harden your hearts as in the rebellion [of Israel], on the day of testing in the wilderness, where your fathers put me to the test and saw my works for forty years. Therefore I was provoked with that generation, and said, 'They always go astray in their hearts; they have not known my ways.' As I swore in my wrath, 'They shall never enter my rest' " (Heb. 3:7–11).

As we look at Israel's history, referred to here, keep in mind that the nation of Israel pictures each one of us in a very personal way. Through the graphic illustration of the victories, trials, and failures of the Hebrew nation, the Holy Spirit means to teach us of God's special love and provision for *us*, as well as to reveal to us the stubbornness of our own hearts.

- What got the Israelites into the wilderness situation? It was unbelief (Heb. 3:19); thus they failed to enter into all that God had made ready for them (pictured by the land of Canaan) to enjoy his rest in the place of spiritual victory.

- Did they have to remain in the wilderness for forty years?

No. It appears that the journey to the promised land could actually have been made in a few weeks.

- Did God know about the obstacles they faced? Yes, and he promised his victory over them.

- What is the name of the leader who finally took Israel into the land? It was Joshua (which means "the Lord God saves").

- What is *your* leader's name? Mine is Jesus, the English equivalent of "Joshua." He is *the Lord God who saves!*

After these sober reminders, the writer of the Hebrews has this word for us: "Let us therefore strive to enter that rest, that no one fall by the same sort of disobedience" (Heb. 4:11).

**Invitation to Rest**

In order to analyze something you usually have to pull it apart or break it down into its basic components. We have just such a situation here: a lot of little pieces labelled "sabbath" lying around, but we have only a vague idea of how they're supposed to fit together again. The one who puts all the pieces together is Jesus. *He* is the New Testament parallel and fulfillment of the sabbath, and he is the reason the sabbath command was not given in the New Testament. Instead of a command, Jesus issues an invitation: "Come to me, all who labor and are heavy laden, and I will give you *rest.* Take my yoke upon you, and learn from me; for I am gentle and lowly in heart, and you will find *rest* for your souls" (Matt. 11:28–29, italics mine).

Our Lord invites all who are tired of going it alone under a heavy load to join up with him. Do you see now what the sabbath is all about? "So then, there remains a sabbath rest [Greek, *sabbatismos,* the only occurrence in the New Testament] for the people of God" (Heb. 4:9). We find our rest by faith in our living Lord! He finds his rest in the obedient and loving response of our hearts as we keep on trusting him! Life is intended to be our enjoying him and his enjoying us!

## Resting While Working

What does the sabbath commandment have to say to us? Is it irrelevant? Far from it; it points up the most vital aspect of Christian life—the rest that comes from counting on the one to whom we're yoked, the Lord Jesus, for every need of our lives. The result, he says, is that ". . . you will find rest for your souls" (Matt. 11:29). The soul, remember, is the emotional, mental, and volitional aspect of our being. Who doesn't need a mind at rest, emotions at peace, and a securely anchored will?

But what's the yoke all about? If you recall, the yoke is a *working* device designed to team up two animals to work together. But what does our Lord promise? He says, ". . . I will give you *rest.*" Do you suppose he could be talking about *resting while working?* Now there's an attractive proposition! All of us have discovered the difference between "work" and "toil." We can be working very intensely at some things and enjoying every minute of it—resting while working. Or we can be really *laboring* at some totally unappealing and odious chore, and hating every minute of it!

What the Lord is offering is a working partnership to make all of life a joy instead of a drag. That's why he says, "For my yoke is easy [pleasant, not harsh] and my burden is light" (Matt. 11:30). As someone has well said, "The rest that Christ offers is not a rest *from* work, but a rest *in* work—not the rest of inactivity, but of harmonious working of all the faculties and affections—of will, heart, imagination, conscience—because each has found in Christ the ideal (and only) sphere for its satisfaction and development" (J. Patrick in *Hastings' Bible Dictionary* and Vine's *Expository Dictionary of the New Testament*).

And how do we do it? We *come* to him and *learn* from him, as he invites us to do. Herein lies the key which unlocks all the abundance of life and joy our hearts desire!

This is what the sabbath is all about, and far from being out of place in the Ten Commandments it has the most far-reaching significance—for Israel and for us. Israel missed God's deeper intent for the sabbath when they took it as bondage instead of blessing. We miss it when we fail to see that the sabbath concept for the Christian is not the observance of a day but rather a 24-hour-a-day, seven-days-a-week resting by faith in the sufficiency of our strong Lord!

## How to Do It Wrong Without Trying

I know a man, a Christian, for whom everything is going wrong: He can't make enough money. . . . He owes everybody. . . . His wife is divorcing him. . . . He's emotionally "all shook up". . . . He's doubting God's goodness. . . . His life is in turmoil. In short, he's not enjoying rest—he's troubled and miserable.

Is God being unfair to him? Doesn't God keep his promise to supply our needs? Is he unfaithful? Oh, there's one thing I failed to mention—he is persisting in a particular sin, sexual immorality, and there is no rest, the Lord says, for the wicked. "Learn from me," he says. But this man isn't listening or learning; he is being just plain wicked! No wonder he has no rest for his soul. No wonder his heart is troubled and his life is a shambles.

Do you see how our choices determine the degree of rest we enjoy? If I walk by faith, I enjoy rest and victory. If I am disobedient, I will end up wandering through a wilderness of troubles and heartaches. We can have it either way. We make the choice.

## Making God Weary

Though God doesn't get tired, we can sure make him

weary. Dr. Willard Aldrich beautifully expounds this theme of the weariness of God:

THE WEARINESS OF GOD

"Does God get tired?

"What could weary 'the everlasting God, the LORD, the Creator of the ends of the earth' who 'does not faint or grow weary' (Isa. 40:20)?

"What could possibly tire the One who created a universe of throbbing energy? Molecules in motion, suns radiating heat, galaxies of heavenly bodies hurtling through space, all bear witness to the boundless energy of Omnipotent God. What could weary such a God?

"The Prophet Isaiah not only reveals that God neither faints nor grows weary but that He renews the strength of those who wait upon Him so that '. . . They shall run and not be weary, they shall walk and not faint' (Isa. 40:31).

"Yet this God is said to be made weary. What can weary God?

"Four things are said to weary God: *Religion that has degenerated into mere form and ceremony wearies God.* The religious observances which He had ordained for ancient Israel, but which were being celebrated without regard to their spiritual significance and moral requirement, were a stench in the nostrils of God. 'Your new moons and your appointed feasts my soul hates; they have become a burden to me, I am weary of bearing them' (Isa. 1:14).

"Could your religion be a weariness to God?

*"God wearies of the unbelief of men who will not hear His Word and trust His promises.* Such is the story of King Ahaz who reigned in Judah about 700 years before Christ's coming into the world. King Ahaz refused to ask for a demonstration of God's power when God through His Prophet Isaiah commanded him to ask for a sign. And Isaiah rebuked his unbelief and disobedience to God by saying, '. . . Is it too little

for you to weary men, that you weary my God also?' (Isa. 7:13).

"Are you guilty of wearying God through your unbelief and disobedience? Have you obeyed God's command to believe on the Lord Jesus Christ? God will judge those '. . . who do not obey the gospel of our Lord Jesus' (2 Thess. 1:8).

"*God grows weary of our sin.* Isaiah charged the nation Israel with wearying God by persistent wickedness. He voiced God's complaint, '. . . you have wearied me with your iniquities' (Isa. 43:24).

"Many voices are being raised today to say that how we live is a matter of indifference. Either God doesn't care, or there isn't a God to care. BUT DO NOT BE DECEIVED BY SUCH DECEITFUL VOICES. There comes a time in God's dealings with men and nations when He so tires of their iniquity that He gives them over to judgment. Preceding the destruction of the world by the flood in the days of Noah, God said, 'My spirit shall not abide in man for ever . . .' (Gen. 6:3).

"*Nothing wearies God more than man's attempts to justify evil conduct.* And the justification of evil is characteristic of the day in which we live. The so-called "new morality" throws off the restraint of God's moral law and judges that evil which is acceptable to society should no longer be considered evil but good. But God wearies of such perversion of moral truth.

"Of this weariness the Prophet Malachi wrote: 'You have wearied the Lord with your words. Yet you say, "How have we wearied him?" By saying, "Every one who does evil is good in the sight of the Lord, and he delights in them." Or by asking, 'Where is the God of justice?" ' (Mal. 2:17).

"Such Divine weariness is a prelude to Divine judgment. Although God is rich in mercy, gracious and longsuffering, not willing that any should perish, yet He grows weary of *religious hypocrisy, unbelieving disobedience, ungodly iniq-*

*uity, and justification of evil* as though it were good.

"It is bad enough to fall into sin. It is proof of deep moral disorder when God's moral standards are distorted so that wrong is called right and evil is considered good.

"Is it possible that God has grown weary of religious formalism, unbelief, wickedness and self-justification in you?" *

The only way we can truly be effective in helping anyone to spiritual victory and emotional stability is by ENTERING GOD'S REST ourselves and then showing others how to do the same. In a world full of turmoil there is a quiet island of peace and confidence in which we can live by trusting the One who said, "COME TO ME" and "I WILL GIVE YOU REST."

Why do we rob ourselves of this rest?

Why do we weary God with our blatant unbelief?

Why do we rob God of *his* rest—in us?

WE DON'T NEED TO! There *is* a rest for the people of God.

## A Question of Intent

We left one open question, of those we posed at the beginning of this study. Why did the Lord Jesus seem to take pains to do his works on the sabbath? And did he break the sabbath law?

First of all, it seems apparent that the one who said he came to *fulfill* the law would hardly act in violation of it. But how do we square this with his actions recorded in John 5:2–18, where he healed a lame man on the sabbath and instructed him to carry his pallet?

We need to observe that the actual instruction given by God through Moses in the law did not forbid either healing

---

* Reprinted by permission of Dr. Willard Aldrich, author and publisher, from *The Doorstep Evangel.*

someone or carrying a mat on the sabbath. But these legalistic Jews, bound by their own additions to what God had said in the law, were quick to accuse the Lord on the basis of their own traditions. So neither of these charges that Jesus violated the sabbath is valid.

But there are also the Lord's own statements on the sabbath: "The sabbath was made for man, not man for the sabbath" (Mark 2:27), and ". . . the Son of man is lord of the sabbath" (Mat. 12:8), and, "So it is lawful to do good on the sabbath" (Mat. 12:12*b*). All of these statements hit at the deeper intent of the sabbath and cut right through the legalistic surface issues.

Going back to John 5, it records ". . . this was why the Jews persecuted Jesus, because he did this on the sabbath" (John 5:16); "But Jesus answered them, 'My Father is working still, and I am working' " (John 5:17). And this brings us full circle. Originally the sabbath was connected with the creative activity of God and his resting to enjoy his creation. Then sin entered and he had to go to work all over again. Then at Sinai, the sabbath was invested with the significance of being a memorial to God's *redemptive* actions in redeeming Israel from slavery in Egypt. In all of this the Jews apparently never caught the real significance and value of *rest*—whether physical or spiritual. Now, the Lord Jesus identifies himself with the Father in his work—work made necessary by the unbelief of man, work dedicated to man's restoration to harmony with the purposes of God—enjoying his rest.

## Jesus, a Sabbath Breaker?

Did our Lord *really* break the sabbath? His own words give us the answer:

> Jesus said to them, "Truly, truly I say to you, the Son can do nothing of his own accord, but only what he sees the Father

doing; for whatever he does, that the Son does likewise" (John 5:19).

Here is one who can say, "I always do what is pleasing to him [the Father]" (John 8:29). That means he keeps perfectly the intent and spirit of the sabbath, for he *always* walked by faith, enjoying the rest of God.

Thus, our Lord is the perfect example of how to keep the sabbath in accord with its original intent and purpose—a fact that is seen by the perfect poise and composure he enjoyed and displayed in his earthly life and ministry. He was never flustered or hurried, not hounded and harried by time and circumstances as we are so often. His life is a perfect exposition of resting by faith in the sufficiency of his Father's loving care!

No wonder he says to us: "Come to me—take my yoke—learn from me—and you will find REST"! For "As the living Father sent me," he says, "and I live because of [by] the Father, so he who eats me [as the bread of life] will live because of [by] me" (John 6:57).

Do you like *life?* Do you appreciate *rest?* They are only available in Jesus Christ.

## Jesus, I Am Resting . . .

The great old hymn says it so well:

> Jesus, I am resting, resting
> In the joy of what thou art;
> I am finding out the greatness
> Of thy loving heart.
>
> Thou hast bid me gaze upon thee,
> And thy beauty fills my soul,
> For by thy transforming power
> Thou hast made me whole.
>
> Oh, how great thy loving kindness,
> Vaster, broader than the sea!

Oh, how marvelous thy goodness,
Lavished all on me!

Simply trusting thee, Lord Jesus,
I behold thee as thou art,
And thy love, so pure, so changeless,
Satisfies my heart.

Ever lift thy face upon me,
As I work and wait for thee;
Resting 'neath thy smile, Lord Jesus,
Earth's dark shadows flee.

Jesus I AM RESTING, resting
In the joy of what thou art,
I am finding out the greatness
Of thy loving heart!*

---

*Jean S. Pigott, 19th century

## CHAPTER FOURTEEN

# Identity and Identification

Perhaps the most crucial problem we face in our day is the restlessness and lostness of a world of men and women who have lost their identity. This is not too surprising when one observes the rapid decay of all the traditional anchor points. The shocking absence of moral standards, the dissolution of the family; thc sad state of the church; the complete lack of integrity in government; the realization of the fact that man has succeeded in polluting large segments of his environment; the dissipation of energy supplies; the wars between nations, sexes, and individuals—all spell out the bankruptcy of human society. No wonder many are feeling so much adrift in a sea of uncertainty that they really don't know who they are!

This identity crisis is not a new phenomenon. I remember some years ago thinking about myself: "How come you think *you* know who *you* are? How can you be so sure of your identity when so many are not?" As a matter of fact, I must confess I was more than a little bit impatient with those who weren't squared away because it seemed so simple to resolve the issue. So I decided to find out how I know who I am. I took a sheet of paper and wrote WHO AM I? at the top and proceeded to fill it out. In doing so I discovered I had to say "in relation to what?" So I ended up with a list of people and things on the left side of the page, with my identity as related to them on the right side. It turned out like this:

## WHO AM I?

My Identity—
Relating to:

| | |
|---|---|
| 1. God . . . | • His creation—made in his image.<br>• His child. He's my loving heavenly Father.<br>• An individual. A one-of-a-kind handmade original, with a God-given personality. I'm *me*. |
| 2. Jesus Christ . . . | • I'm his, for he bought me with a price—his life.<br>• I'm accepted in him. He loves me without reservation or qualification, with an everlasting love! |
| 3. The Holy Spirit . . . | • I'm indwelt by him, regenerated by him, sealed by him: made safe and secure under God's ownership. |
| 4. My Family . . . | • I'm Pearl Smith's husband, responsible to provide the leadership of love toward her.<br>• I'm Don and Dave's dad, enjoying a man-to-man relationship with them as my two grown sons. |
| 5. God's Family . . . | • A member of the greatest family in heaven and on earth! Joined to every other member of the body of Christ, worldwide. Enjoying the privilege of fellowship with many of God's own. |
| 6. Other People . . . At work, etc. | • Relating to a great bunch of choice folks in a loving church fellowship.<br>• Enjoying wonderful fellowship with fellow workers, fellow elders and pastors.<br>• Meeting more of God's dear people all the time. |

| | |
|---|---|
| 7. In Time . . . | • I'm a man under construction—just in process, not a finished product, but learning.<br>• Possessor of eternal, abundant life in Christ.<br>• Joint heir with Christ of all that's his. |
| 8. In Eternity . . . | • I'll receive the fullness of my inheritance: a resurrection body, knowing as I am known, glorified, experiencing the glorious liberty of the sons of God, conformed to the image of God's Son! |

THAT'S WHO I AM! HOW GOOD CAN IT GET?

This listing is not exhaustive but merely suggests how anyone may discover his or her identity. The result for me was very solidifying and satisfying. But notice: most of the information I used to establish my identity was from the Scriptures. All I did was to review the information God had given me in his Word. So it's not surprising that those who don't know or believe the truth of God have trouble knowing who they are.

## Adam or Christ?

This leads us to the matter of *identification,* a very important consideration both for us and for those we counsel. Here again I turn to the Bible and find that I am either identified *with Adam* or *with Christ.* If one has not yet claimed Jesus Christ as Savior, he is still in Adam and thus heir to all that means: a fallen, depraved nature, condemnation, frustration, futility, death.

On the other hand if I have received Christ, I am identified with him and made partaker of a new nature, the divine nature. I think it is more easily seen in chart form, like this:

MY IDENTIFICATION WITH CHRIST

| | |
|---|---|
| In His Death | • *He died for me* (Rom. 5:8).<br>This means fullness of pardon, forgiveness, acceptance.<br>• *I died with him* (Rom. 6:6).<br>This puts the old man out of business—frees me from what I was in Adam, a slave to sin. |
| In His Burial | • *I was buried with him* (Rom. 6:4).<br>This means that if I want to relate to the old man, I'll have to dig him up. |
| In His Risen Life | • *I live with him* in newness of life (Rom. 6:4*b*–5).<br>The old way of sin and death has no more claim on me. |
| In His Glory | • *I share the splendor of his character, by his indwelling life* (John 17:22, 2 Cor. 4:7, Rom. 8:17,18).<br>My humanity is fulfilled as he lives in me and makes me the man I want to be. |
| In His Concern for a Lost World | • *I have been sent as his ambassador to share his good news with a world that does not know him* (John 17:18, 20, 2 Cor. 5:19–21).<br>Wherever I go, he goes—so I am his representative—a high calling and responsibility. |
| In His Triumph | • *He always leads me in triumph* (2 Cor. 2:14).<br>• Over sin (Rom. 6:14).<br>• Over circumstances (Rom. 8:25–28).<br>• Over Satan (Col. 2:15). |
| In His Reign | • *I am to reign in life through him* (Rom. 5:17).<br>This is for the present. |

| | |
|---|---|
| | • *I will reign with him*—in the future (Rev. 5:10). |
| As Joint Heir with Him | • *Sharing in all that is his* (Rom. 8:14, 17). This means more than I can even comprehend, for his Word says, "All things are yours, and you are Christ's, and Christ is God's" (1 Cor. 3:21–23). |
| But Also—In His Suffering | • This is part of the package, for we are heirs ". . . provided we suffer with him in order that we may also be glorified with him (Rom. 8:17*b*, also Phil. 1:29 and 1 Pet. 4:12–13). |

The living out of all that this identification affords makes for a very exciting and worthwhile life. Why? Because it is the life of Jesus (the life of the ages) being manifested in us.

But notice that it is life out of death. We must be DYING TO LIVE!

> . . . unless a grain of wheat falls into the earth and dies, it remains alone; but if it dies, it bears much fruit. He who loves his life loses it, and he who hates his life in this world will keep it for eternal life (John 12:24–25).

> . . . always carrying in the body the *death* of Jesus, so that the *life* of Jesus may also be manifested in our bodies. For while we live we are always being given up to death for Jesus' sake, so that the *life* of Jesus may be manifested in our mortal flesh. So *death* is at work in us, but *life* in you (2 Cor. 4:10–12, italics mine).

This is the truth we must live and share with those God calls us to help—the many around us who are dying to live.

WOULD YOU CONSIDER....

# INDEX TO THE APPENDIX

**Acknowledgement**

The fine work of Charlotte Mersereau, Paul Leavenworth and my fellow pastor, Brian Morgan, is much appreciated. We want to express our thanks for permission to use their materials and for helpful insights gained from others of my Christian friends in our mutual learning experience.

APPENDIX A

# Spiritual Principles of Counseling

By Paul Leavenworth

| Forms of Sin/Definition | Results | Scriptural Solution | Results | Scriptural Ref. |
|---|---|---|---|---|
| Sin—*hamartía*, "a missing of the mark"—basic attitude of trying to live life without God. | Death—Romans 6:23 | Confession—*homologeō*, "to speak the same thing"—call it what it is. | Forgiveness Cleansing | 1 John 1:9 |
| Alienation—*appallotrióv*, means foreign, strange, not of one's own family, alien, an enemy. | No Hope and without God in this world—Ephesians 2:12 | Knowing Jesus Christ Ephesians 2:13. | Fellowship Peace Ephesians 2:13–14. | Ephesians 2:12, 4:18 Colossians 1:21 |
| Anger—*orgē*, "originally any natural impulse, or desire, or disposition . . . as the strongest of all passion," emotion of displeasure. | Guilt—Matthew 5:22—imprisonment | Confession—Ephesians 4:26. anger relates directly to personal rights we feel we have. | Freedom | Ephesians 4:26, 31 Matthew 5:22 |

| Forms of Sin/Definition | Results | Scriptural Solution | Results | Scriptural Ref. |
| --- | --- | --- | --- | --- |
| Argument (strife, quarreling)—*éris,* "exertion or contention for superiority" (Webster). | Disorder—chaos James 3:16, 1 Timothy 6:3 | Humility of Mind, let each of you regard one as more important than himself, Philippians 2:3. | Understanding | Galatians 5:20<br>Philippians 2:3<br>James 3:14, 16 |
| Bitterness—*pikría,* from a root *pik,* meaning to cut to prick . . . pointed, sharp pungent to the sense of taste, smell, etc. | Bondage to iniquity Acts 8:23 | Seek ye *first* the kingdom of God and his righteousness, Matthew 6:33. | Wisdom from above, James 3:17–18. | Ephesians 4:31<br>Hebrews 12:15<br>James 3:11, 14 |
| Blaming—"to hold responsible," Webster—placing responsibility of our actions upon others. | Irresponsibility not dealing with the problem | Becoming Blameless in Christ Jesus (I am the problem). *ámōmos,* unblemished; *ámemptos,* unblamed. | Light—Philippians 2:15 | Philippians 2:15<br>1 Thessalonians 3:13 |
| Boasting—*kaucháomai,* to glory, to build up one's own | Insecurity not realistic self-image. | Boasting in God—1 Corinthians 1:31. | Security—basis of proper self- | Ephesians 2:8–9<br>2 Corinthians 1:31<br>2 Corinthians 12:9 |

| self-importance, sufficiency, etc. | | | image is reality. | |
|---|---|---|---|---|
| LACK OF COMMUNICATION—opposite of *koinonéo,* "a having in common," "a process by which meanings are exchanged between individuals through a common system of symbols" (Webster). | MISUNDERSTANDING Romans 3:11; alienation from God, men and self. | COMMUNICATION comes from a right relationship with God, Genesis 3. God is the author of communication. SIN destroyed it. | UNDERSTANDING | Psalm 119:104<br>Hebrews 11:3, Exodus 4:10–12 (Moses' tongue)<br>James 1:19 ("quick to hear, slow to speak")<br>Proverbs 15:2 |
| CONFUSION—*akatastasía,* "down standing," instability, a state of disorder, unsureness of condition or direction. | DISORDER AND EVERY EVIL THING, James 3:16. | Need to ask God if there is SIN in our life—if so, confess; if not, wait upon him. | PEACE, STABILITY | 1 Corinthians 14:33<br>James 1:5–8, 3:16<br>Matthew 7:24–27 |
| COMPLAINING (dissatisfaction)—*mempsímolros,* finding fault with one's lot, hence, discontented, quarrelous—not content. | BITTERNESS, INGRATITUDE NEGATIVE ATTITUDE | Christ is sufficient to meet our every need. (Note difference between *need* and *want*), Philippians 4:11–13. | SATISFACTION Matthew 5:6 | Jude 16<br>Philippians 4:11–13<br>Matthew 6:33 |

| Forms of Sin/Definition | Results | Scriptural Solution | Results | Scriptural Ref. |
|---|---|---|---|---|
| Distrust (fear)—*phóbos,* a slavish fear of a master or a criminal's fear of a judge (Wuest)—distrusting God. | Guilt (dread of punishment). | Love—*agapaō* 1 Corinthians 13. | Confidence 1 John 4:17 | 1 John 4:18 |
| Despair (depression)—*exaporéomai,* "to have no outlet whatever, to be at a loss, without resource." | Depression (emotionally drained). | Acceptance of trials, to produce Christ-like character. Depression is usually a result of unattained expectations. | Hope—perplexed but not despairing, 2 Corinthians 4:8 | 2 Corinthians 4:7–11<br>James 1:2–4<br>Romans 5:3–5 |
| Disputes (dissension, war)—conflict involving words, ideas, actions, etc. | Constant Friction between men, 1 Timothy 6:5. | Humility—James 4:10. | Honor—to be exalted, "raised up," Proverbs 15:33. | 2 Corinthians 4:7–11<br>James 1:2–4<br>Romans 5:3–5 |
| Envy—*phthónos,* "a feeling of displeasure produced by witnessing or hearing of the advantage or prosperity | Insecurity—Wrong value system.<br>Bitternesss—Because we can't have | Fulfillment, having God's value system—Matthew 6:33; "hunger and thirst after right- | Satisfaction—"filled to the brim." | Proverbs 23:17–18<br>Titus 3:3–7<br>1 Peter 2:1–3, "word." |

| of others," produced by a desire to have the same thing. | what we think we should, James 3:11–16. | eousness," Matthew 5:6. | | |
|---|---|---|---|---|
| FALSE EXPECTATIONS —*apokarodokía,* "watching with outstretched head," "reaching out in readiness to receive something." | DISAPPOINTMENT— people and things can never live up to our expectations. | RESIGNATION—Not my will but thine be done, Luke 22:42. | REST—Hebrews 4:10. | Isaiah 55:8–9<br>Psalm 37:4–5 |
| FRUSTRATION—*athetéō,* "to put aside," "failing to define our responsibilities or our priorities or failing to put our whole heart into achieving them" (Bill Gothard). | DISCOURAGEMENT—not fulfilling goals, thus not fulfilling self. | Proper PRIORITIES (defining responsibilities), Luke 10:38–42. | SATISFIED Matthew 5:6. | Galatians 2:21, "nullify."<br>Galatians 6:2–9 |
| FUTILITY—*matalótēs* (vanity), "emptiness as to results," lack of meaning and purpose. | SLAVERY to corruption, 2 Peter 2:18. | RENEWING the spirit of our mind to see life from God's point of view, Ephesians 4:23–24. | RIGHTEOUSNESS and HOLINESS, Ephesians 4:24. | Acts 14:15<br>Romans 8:20<br>Ephesians 4:17–24<br>Ecclesiastes 12:13 |

| Forms of Sin/Definition | Results | Scriptural Solution | Results | Scriptural Ref. |
|---|---|---|---|---|
| Fear—see Distrust | | | | |
| Gossip—*diábolos,* "false accusers, slanderers," used 34 times in N.T. as the title of Satan, "sharing private information about others with those that are not part of the problem or the solution" (Gothard). | Restless Evil and full of deadly Poison, James 3:8. Disorder—James 3:15–16 (hurt, misunderstanding). | Speaking the Truth in Love—Ephesians 4:15 good for edification, Ephesians 4:29. | Grace—Ephesians 4:29. | 1 Peter 3:16–22, insult, harass<br>2 Timothy 3:3<br>Titus 2:3<br>Proverbs 15:1–2<br>Matthew 18:15–17<br>1 Timothy 5:19–22 |
| Greed—Covetousness (*pleonexía*), "a desire to have more, always in a bad sense." | Dissatisfaction—insecurity because our values are based on that which is unstable. | Thankfulness—*charis,* basic Greek root, putting our eyes on what we do have instead of what we don't. | Joy—Satisfaction, Matthew 5:6. | Romans 1:29<br>Ephesians 5:3–4, "thanks"<br>Colossians 3:1–5<br>Matthew 5:6, "satisfied." |
| Guilt—*énochos,* "held in, bound by, liable to a change or action at law," or "the fact of | Fear—Alienation | Sacrifice—Romans 3:19–26, "justifier of the one who has faith in Jesus." | Clean—Free—John 8:31–36—Life, Romans 6:23. | Romans 3:19–26 |

| | | | | |
|---|---|---|---|---|
| having committed a breach of conduct especially violating a law and involving penalty" (Webster). | | | | |
| HATRED—enmity (*échthra*), the opposite of agape, "love." *Miseō,* malicious and unjustifiable feelings toward others," desire to destroy because someone or something stands in the way of what you want. | MURDER—1 John 3:15. | LOVE—we need to die to our desires in order to meet the needs of others, 1 John 3:16, 18. | PEACE, Ephesias 2:15. | Romans 8:7<br>James 4:4 |
| IMPATIENCE—opposite of *hupomonē,* an abiding under. "Restlessness of spirit, as under irritation, delay or opposition" (Webster). | RESTLESSNESS—WORRY | FAITH in the promises of God, Romans 8:25. | MATURITY | Romans 5:3–5<br>James 1:2–5<br>Hebrews 16:36<br>Romans 8:25<br>2 Peter 3:9 |
| IDOLATRY—*cidolōlatriá,* an idolater is a slave to the | DEPRAVITY—Romans 1: 18–32. | HONOR Him and give THANKS, Romans 1:21. | LIBERTY, 2 Corinthians 3:17. | 1 Corinthians 10:6–7, 14<br>Colossians 3:5 |

| Forms of Sin/Definition | Results | Scriptural Solution | Results | Scriptural Ref. |
|---|---|---|---|---|
| depraved ideas his idol represents, "serving the creature rather than the creator," Romans 1:25. | Materialism is a common form today. | | | |
| Immorality—(lust) (sensuality) *epithuméo,* "to fix the desire upon." *Pleonexía,* "the desire to have more always in a bad sense, inconsistent with purity or good morals" (Webster). | Callousness—Ephesians 4:19. | Sanctification—"Put to its proper use." Deal with lust before it is conceived, producing death, James 1:13–15; Matthew 5:27–28. | Fulfillment | 1 Thessalonians 4:3–7<br>James 1:13–15 |
| Inferiority—*hēttáomai,* "to be less," "comparing our appearance, abilities, parentage or social heritage with that of others" (Gothard ALI). | Insecurity<br>Alienation | Reality—learning to value ourselves as God sees us, 1 Peter 2:9; Psalm 139:13–16. | Acceptance<br>Confidence | 2 Corinthians 12:13<br>2 Corinthians 10:12 |
| Insecurity—The opposite of *hikanós* | Possessiveness | Security comes through a life | Stability | Matthew 7:24–27<br>Romans 8:35–39 |

| | | | | |
|---|---|---|---|---|
| (security, sufficiency). Insecurity is "building our life and affections around someone or something we know can be taken away from us" (Gothard ALI). | | founded upon the ROCK, Jesus Christ, and obedience to his Word. | | |
| IRRESPONSIBILITY—trying to take what we feel is a shortcut to our goals. | MANIPULATION<br>INSTABILITY | SUBMISSION—Jesus didn't take what seemed to be the shortcut but was obedient, even unto death, 2 Peter 2:18–24. | EXALTATION, 1 Peter 5:6. | Psalm 107:7<br>Matthew 4:8–11<br>Matthew 5:6; 6:33 |
| INSENSITIVITY—Lacking compassion (several Greek words): *splanchnízomai,* "to be moved as to one's inwards"; *sumpathéō,* "to suffer with another"; *eleéō,* "to have mercy, to show kindness, by bene- | MISUNDERSTANDING<br>HURT | View others as MORE IMPORTANT than myself, Philippians 2:3. | UNITY, Colossians 3:14. Love is the perfect bond of unity. | Philippians 2:1–11<br>Colossians 3:12–17<br>Galatians 6:2 |

| Forms of Sin/Definition | Results | Scriptural Solution | Results | Scriptural Ref. |
|---|---|---|---|---|
| Insensitivity (cont.) ficence or assistance," to view my needs as more important than another's, Philippians 2:3. | | | | |
| Jealousy—*zēlóō,* "to seek or desire to deprive another of pleasure which draws him away from you" (Bill Gothard). | Possessiveness | Serving—seeking to edify our brothers, Hebrews 16:24. | Simplicity and Purity, 2 Corinthians 11:2–3 | Proverbs 6:34<br>Hebrews 10:24–25<br>2 Corinthians 11:2–3 |
| Loneliness—*mónos,* "single, alone, solitary," sense of separation from others. | Self-Pity | Death—willingness to *serve* others, to produce fruit in their lives, not demanding my desires be met. | Fruitfulness | John 12:24 |
| Pride—*tuphóō,* "to wrap in smoke" (from *tuphos,* smoke; metaphori- | Strife—Proverbs 13:10.<br>Destruction—Proverbs | Humility—seeing myself as God sees me, 1 Peter 5:6. | Honor—Proverbs 15:33 | 1 Timothy 3:6<br>1 John 2:16 |

| cally, for conceit), to view yourself more important than you ought, Romans 12:3, 16. | 16:18. | | | |
|---|---|---|---|---|
| REBELLION—(Heb. *marah* means "to be or make bitter"), reference many times to rebellion against God's commandments. | INSECURITY—Defying the only foundation that can hold me up. | BROKEN WILL—so that His will is my will, Psalm 51:17. | STABILITY, SATISFACTION—Matthew 5:6 Ephesians 6:10–20 Matthew 7:24–27 | Psalm 23:4<br>Proverbs 10:13; 13, 24; 22:15; 23:13–14; 29:15, "rod." |
| RESENTMENT—"feeling of indignant displeasure at something regarded as wrong, insult or injury" (Webster). | MISUNDERSTANDING, LACK OF COMMUNICATION—Proverbs 18:19. | Willingness to be hurt or misunderstood for God's glory. DEATH to the old man. | HEALING—1 Peter 2:24. | 2 Timothy 2:24–26<br>1 Peter 2:18–25<br>2 Corinthians 5:10 |
| REVENGE—*ekdikéō,* "one who exacts a penalty from a person," attempting to hurt someone in return for hurting me (or someone close to me). | WAR—James 4:1–10. It takes two to make a fight. | HUMILITY—giving our hurt over to God, James 4:10. | HONOR and HEALING | James 4:1–10<br>Romans 12:19<br>Hebrews 10:30 |

| Forms of Sin/Definition | Results | Scriptural Solution | Results | Scriptural Ref. |
|---|---|---|---|---|
| SELFISHNESS—*authádēs,* "self-pleasing," dominated by self-interest and inconsiderate to others, arrogantly asserting his own will. | DESTRUCTION—2 Peter 2:12. | Being a GOD-PLEASER, not a man-pleaser, Colossians 3:23; Ephesians 6:6–7. | GOOD—Ephesians 6:8. | Titus 1:7<br>2 Peter 2:10<br>Psalm 37:4–5 |
| SHAME—*aischúnē,* "shame, nakedness," "a painful emotion caused by consciousness of guilt . . ." (Webster). | FEAR, UNCLEANNESS, as an expression of guilt feelings. | Need for RESTORATION through confession of SIN. | FORGIVENESS, CLEANSING | 1 John 1:9 |
| TRANSGRESS—N.T. *parábasis,* primarily a going aside then, an overstepping (always of a breach of law). | BITTERNESS—Blaming God for insecurity. | Process God uses is a rod of correction, Hebrews 12:5–16, "discipline." | | |
| UNGRATEFULNESS—opposite of *eucharistía,* "that which | CYNICISM, BITTERNESS—Romans 1: | THANKFULNESS—Philippians 4:6. Seeking to | JOY<br>PEACE—Philippians 4:7 | Romans 1:21<br>2 Corinthians 4:15<br>Ephesians 5:4 |

| | | | | |
|---|---|---|---|---|
| bestows or occasions pleasure, delight, or causes favorable regard." Looking at what I don't have, rather than rejoicing in what I do have. | 18–33. | see God's positive love in all things. | | |
| WORRY—*mérimna,* probably connected with *merizo,* to draw in different directions, distract . . . a distracting care, "assuming responsibilities God never intended us to have" (Bill Gothard). | IRRITATION IMPATIENCE | PRIORITIES of responsibilities (need to define responsibilities), walking by faith in God's promises. | REST—Hebrews 4:16 | Philippians 4:6–7<br>Matthew 6:33–34<br>Hebrews 4:10 |

1) Basic Greek definitions from *Vine's Expository Dictionary.*
2) Webster's Seventh New College Dictionary.
3) "Operational Definitions," Advanced Leadership Institute, Bill Gothard.

# APPENDIX B

# Sins and Solutions

By Charlotte Mersereau

| Problem | Answer | Redemptive Biblical Solution |
| --- | --- | --- |
| 1. Guilt | Forgiveness<br>Forgetting<br>Admission | 1 John 1:9<br>Philippians 3:13–14<br>Psalm 51 |
| 2. Inadequacy | Acceptance | Psalm 139:14<br>Ephesians 1:6, 6:10<br>Colossians 2:10*a*<br>2 Corinthians 12:9 |
| 3. Blame shifting | Confession<br>Truth, reality | 1 John 1:9<br>Psalm 51:1–4 |
| 4. Slavery to self, world system, "things" | Family relationship | Romans 8:15–16<br>1 John 3:1–2<br>Galatians 3:26 |
| 5. Depression | Riches in Christ | Romans 8:17<br>1 Corinthians 4:8<br>Philippians 4:19 |
| 6. Rebelliousness | Submissiveness | James 4:7*a*, 8*a*, 10*a*<br>Ephesians 5:21<br>Hebrews 13:17; 1 Peter 2:13 |
| 7. Frustration and futility | Peace | 1 Corinthians 14:33*a*<br>Isaiah 32:17 |
| 8. Operation "feeling" | Facts | Job 19:25<br>2 Timothy 1:12<br>Philippians 1:6 |
| 9. Doubt | Assurance (Security) | Jude 1:1, 24<br>John 10:28<br>Romans 5:8, 9; 8:38–39<br>Philippians 1:6<br>1 Peter 1:3–5 |
| 10. Idleness | Investment | Ephesians 2:10<br>2 Timothy 3:16–17 |

| Problem | Answer | Redemptive Biblical Solution |
| --- | --- | --- |
| 11. Suffering | Healing/restoration, Truth | 1 Peter 1:6, 7; 4:12–13, 16 |
| | Self-judgment (disciplinary) | James 1:2–4, 12 |
| | | 1 Peter 4:17–19 |
| | | 1 Corinthians 11:31–32 |
| | | Hebrews 12:5–13 |
| 12. Spiritual death | Life | John 1:4; 3:36; 5:26 |
| | Salvation | John 3:3–15 |
| | | 2 Corinthians 5:17 |
| | | Ephesians 2:1, 5 |
| | | Revelation 2:11 |
| 13. Physical death | Eternal Life | 2 Corinthians 5:1–8 |
| | Resurrection | 1 Corinthians 15:42–44 |
| | | 2 Corinthians 5:1–8 |
| | | 1 Thessalonians 4:14–18 |
| | Comfort | Matthew 5:4, Psalm 84:1–2, 4 |
| | | Revelation 14:13, Psalm 116:15 |
| 14. Slavery | Freedom | 2 Corinthians 3:17 |
| | | John 8:31–32, 36 |
| | | Galatians 5:1 |
| 15. Anxiety | Peace | Philippians 4:6, 7 |
| | | Matthew 6:25–34 |
| | | Hebrews 13:5–6 |
| 16. Submission | Obedience | Colossians 3:18–20, 22, 23 |
| 17. Wall building "cover up" | Self-Acceptance | Ephesians 1:6 |
| | | Colossians 2:10 |
| 18. "Lovers of Self" | Dying with Christ | 2 Corinthians 4:10–12 |
| 19. Temptations/trials | Discernment | 1 Corinthians 10:13 |
| | Power | |
| | Truth | |
| 20. Awareness of good and evil | Discernment | Colossians 3:1–3, 16 |
| | Disciplined mind | Psalm 139:17–18 |
| | | Proverbs 16:3 |

| | PROBLEM | ANSWER | REDEMPTIVE BIBLICAL SOLUTION |
|---|---|---|---|
| 21. | Identity crisis | True identity | Colossians 2:10<br>Psalm 139:14–16 |
| 22. | Living in a world of illusion | Reality/truth | Joshua 1:8<br>John 8:31–32 |
| 23. | Isolation/ loneliness | Communication; God<br>Communication; Man | 1 John 1:7<br>Romans 8:1<br>Colossians 3:12–14<br>1 Corinthians 13 |
| 24. | "Cop out" to escape consequences | Confession | 1 John 1:9<br>Psalm 139:23–24 |
| 25. | Ego trip | Truth: death of old man | 2 Corinthians 5:15; 4:5–7, 10–12; 3:5 |
| 26. | Loneliness | Family relationship<br>Friend | 1 John 3:1–2<br>John 15:15 |
| 27. | Hate | Love | John 13–35<br>Romans 13:8<br>Matthew 5:44 |
| 28. | Anger | Forgiveness<br>Forgetting | Philippians 2:5–8<br>Colossians 3:10–14 |
| 29. | Thanklessness | Thankfulness | Colossians 3:15, 17<br>Ephesians 1:20<br>1 Thessalonians 5:18<br>Philippians 4:6 |

# APPENDIX C

# Saul and David: The Man of the Flesh and the Man of Faith

By Brian Morgan

## A. Principles Observed in the Man of the Flesh

(A study in the life of Saul)
(1 Samuel 8–31)

- The flesh takes the activity of God and keeps it outwardly religious but interjects the principles of the world within (1 Sam. 8:5; 2 Tim. 3:5, 9).
- The desire of the flesh is to use God for its own advancement rather than to serve him (1 Sam. 10:16–21).
- A life of failure and defeat because of the dominance of the flesh is usually due to *disobedience, not ignorance* (1 Sam. 9:25; 10:13; Rom. 1:18).
- The flesh can look great in the beginning with external glory, but that glory ultimately fades away (1 Sam. 10:23–24, 11:15; 2 Cor. 3:11).
- The flesh thrives on outward security and favorable circumstances (2 Cor. 4:18).
- The man of the flesh depends upon himself until he gets in trouble. Then he calls upon God, but still does not fully desire God's way; he only wants help to alleviate the circumstance (1 Sam. 13:8–14).
- Upon rejection by God and a loss of authority, the flesh responds by stirring up all kinds of religious activity and involvement (1) to cover up the rejection and (2) because it believes that outward activity has some kind of power in and of itself (1 Sam. 14:3, 24, 35; Gal. 3:1–3).
- The flesh presumes to find good in what God has called utterly bad (1 Sam. 15:9).
- The flesh will applaud itself and take credit for the activity of God (1 Sam. 15:12).
- The flesh, in an attempt to keep something which God has denounced, will dedicate it to God. It will do anything to stay alive—even be religious (1 Sam. 15:15).
- The flesh rationalizes sin and will even make conditional repentance but will never fully repent—i.e., to call sin, sin; for to do so it would have to die (1 Sam. 15:25, 30).

- Allowing a little flesh to live in our lives will lead to further disobedience, rebellion, and rejection of God's Word and authority on our part, and on God's part a grieving of his Spirit and a withdrawal of his power, authority, and truth in our lives (1 Sam. 15:35).
- The flesh will always come in conflict with the Spirit (1 Sam. 18–30; Gal. 4:29).
- The man of the flesh may be melted by the love of another, but often it is only an emotion: emotion that does not lead to obedience is useless and will lead to deeper sin and rebellion (1 Sam. 24:16–22, 26; 17–25).
- In the course of time the man of the flesh (knowing of his doom) will ultimately come into open rebellion against God and battle God to man's death (1 Sam. 20:31, 22:7; 2 Tim. 3:8–9).
- The man of the flesh is sorry for the consequences of sin, will fear them and even try to manipulate them, but is never sorry for sin itself (1 Sam. 28:5).
- The end to which the flesh leads is utter depravity, barrenness, witchcraft, and finally suicide. When we submit to the flesh we are in fact for that moment committing spiritual suicide. "The wages of sin is death" (1 Sam. 31:4, Rom. 6:23).

### B. Principles Observed in the Man of Faith
(A study in the life of David)
(1 Samuel 16—2 Samuel 1)

- God's chosen are recognized by their heart response to God, not by outward appearance or activity.
- The man of faith is not put on the throne immediately but is tested by struggle and adversity until at last he learns the principle that man can do nothing on his own, learning the fullness of God's provision *even in exile*.
- Faith never looks at outward circumstances but upon God for victory.
- The man of faith does not work out God's program on his own or take things into his own hands, but waits for God to work it out and keeps entrusting himself to God to judge his circumstances rightly.
- The man of faith will hold to God's promises even when circumstances seem exactly the opposite to them.
- The man of faith can sin and fail, but the difference between him and the man of the flesh is real *repentance* and submission to God to be Lord of his life.

APPENDIX D

# Repentance—The False and the True, As Seen in Saul and David

By Brian Morgan

| KING* | SIN | RESULT | ULTIMATE END |
|---|---|---|---|
| SAUL'S STORY | DISOBEDIENCE: offered the burnt offering, intruding into an area not assigned to him. | Lost his *Kingdom*—his area of authority and responsibility, his influence on the nation. | Instead of repentance, he increased his religious activity to gain back his lost authority. |
| | INDULGENCE: allowed the flesh (Amalekites) to live, against God's commands. | Lost his right to be *King*. Because he refused to crucify the flesh he became a SLAVE TO SIN (Rom. 6:16), not free to choose any longer. God's Spirit leaves him to his own devices. | Only *conditional* repentance—"I sinned, but . . ." Only sorry for the consequences of sin, turns to witchcraft to deal with the problem; then, *not being able to face the consequences he commits suicide.* |

* king—"melekh"— (decider or counselor) —one who chooses, thus a picture of our human will.

| King | Sin | Result | Ultimate End |
|---|---|---|---|
| David's Story | Adultery and Murder | The sword never departed from his house—lost his authority and influence in his *kingdom.* | *Repented* (Psalm 51), therefore he maintained his right to be king. David was *restored but still had to face the consequences of his sin.* |

## APPENDIX E

# How's Your Mental Health?

(A Personal Inventory)

Check one space to answer each question: (1) __ (2) __ (3) __ (4) __

(1) Not at all (or "it's not")
(2) Sometimes (or "just fair")
(3) Pretty consistently (or consistently good)
(4) None of your business.

---

1. How well can you take rejection? (1) __ (2) __ (3) __ (4) __
2. How does your love hold up in the face of rebuffs? (1) __ (2) __ (3) __ (4) __
3. How panic-proof are you in the face of pressures? (1) __ (2) __ (3) __ (4) __
4. How well can you take injury without resentment? (1) __ (2) __ (3) __ (4) __
5. How well can you handle praise without pride? (1) __ (2) __ (3) __ (4) __
6. Do you generally have a good sense of personal worth? (1) __ (2) __ (3) __ (4) __
7. How realistic is your assessment of your own importance? (1) __ (2) __ (3) __ (4) __
8. Are you able to relate objectively to the needs of others? (1) __ (2) __ (3) __ (4) __
9. Are you available to be part of the solution in most every problem situation? (1) __ (2) __ (3) __ (4) __
10. Are you at rest in the midst of a world in turmoil? (1) __ (2) __ (3) __ (4) __
11. Are you steadfastly committed to right causes and right actions? (1) __ (2) __ (3) __ (4) __
12. Are you cheerfully optimistic even when all seems lost? (1) __ (2) __ (3) __ (4) __
13. Do you have a clear sense of direction in a confused world? (1) __ (2) __ (3) __ (4) __
14. Are you free from guilt (either real or false)? (1) __ (2) __ (3) __ (4) __

15. Are you free from being plagued by regrets? (1) __ (2) __ (3) __ (4) __
16. Are you free from being blackmailed by fears? (1) __ (2) __ (3) __ (4) __
17. Are your priorities generally in order? (1) __ (2) __ (3) __ (4) __
18. Do you have a good sense of humor (especially when the joke is on you)? (1) __ (2) __ (3) __ (4) __
19. How well do you "hang in there" when the going gets tough? (1) __ (2) __ (3) __ (4) __
20. How non-defensive is your attitude? (1) __ (2) __ (3) __ (4) __
21. How open are you to correction? (1) __ (2) __ (3) __ (4) __
22. How emotionally stable are you? (1) __ (2) __ (3) __ (4) __
23. Are you a confident person? (1) __ (2) __ (3) __ (4) __
24. How well do you handle suffering? (1) __ (2) __ (3) __ (4) __
25. How teachable are you? (1) __ (2) __ (3) __ (4) __
26. How vulnerable are you willing to be? (1) __ (2) __ (3) __ (4) __
27. How transparent and open are you? (1) __ (2) __ (3) __ (4) __
28. How good is your balance between liberty and license? (1) __ (2) __ (3) __ (4) __
29. How well do you "keep going" without encouragement? (1) __ (2) __ (3) __ (4) __
30. How submissive are you to authority? (1) __ (2) __ (3) __ (4) __
31. How effective is your leadership? (1) __ (2) __ (3) __ (4) __
32. How fulfilling is your value system? (1) __ (2) __ (3) __ (4) __
33. How well adjusted is your attitude toward the opposite sex? (1) __ (2) __ (3) __ (4) __
34. How free are you from indulging in emotional thinking? (1) __ (2) __ (3) __ (4) __
35. How willing are you to forego your rights? (1) __ (2) __ (3) __ (4) __

TOTALS (1) __ (2) __ (3) __ (4) __

No fair peeking at the scoring sheet until you've answered all the questions!

# MENTAL HEALTH INVENTORY SCORING SHEET

- *Add up all the 1's, 2's and 3's,* using the number values; that is, if you checked 3, add 3; if you checked 2, add 2, and so on. If your total score is *between 70 and 100,* you're doing great —keep it up! If you scored between 35 and 69, you've got a lot of learning and growing to do!

- *Now add up all the 4's.*
  Any score over 12 indicates that you are probably defending these areas, not letting Christ be Lord. You may find it helpful to review each of the questions on which you marked 4 and consciously yield that area to Christ for correction.

  If you have a score of 70 or more as a total of all your 4's, you should question whether you *have ever made Christ your Lord.*

Perhaps you've noticed that on all these questions Jesus Christ scored perfectly—100 percent! He is the model of perfect mental health, always poised, unhurried, loving and confident. Since he lives in every Christian, he will supply the motivation and power in each of his own to respond rightly with increasing consistency. Mental health is simply experiencing the normal Christian life.

For example, regarding question number 1, the Lord Jesus was "despised and rejected by men" (Isa. 53:3), and "forsaken by the Father" (Ps. 22:1); yet "he trusted to him who judges justly" (1 Peter 3:23), and by faith handled total and utter rejection.

We are to follow in his steps (1 Pet. 3:21). You can think it through in regard to every issue.

"... we have the mind of Christ" (1 Cor. 2:16*b*).

---

Scoring is purely arbitrary and is designed simply to help you assess your responses—then turn to the Lord for the indicated correction and strength.

# APPENDIX F
# Further Facts about the Flesh

## *PUTTING OFF AND PUTTING ON*

We need to observe that dealing with the flesh involves two steps: a negative and a positive. It is *putting off* and *putting on,* and we must take the negative step first. Often we do it wrong by trying to move to the positive first. We have a problem with the flesh and say, "I'll just leave it with the Lord; I'll trust the Lord to handle it." Then we wonder why we are not helped. First you must *put off,* then *put on.* In both Ephesians and Colossians we have instruction to "put off the old man and to put on the new man." It's just as if we were divesting ourselves of an old garment that is tattered, dirty, worn, and outmoded and were putting on a new garment. The Scripture is consistent that the negative precedes the positive. Note the order in Romans: "Our old man died with Christ" (Rom. 6:6), but he also *"lives* with Christ in resurrection power" (Rom. 6:8). The negative: Romans 6:6, "We know that our old self was crucified with him so that the sinful body might be destroyed." The positive: Romans 6:8, "But if we have died with Christ, we believe that we also shall live with him." It is "life out of death"—dying in order to live. It isn't dying just to die. Nobody's dying to die, but we *are* dying to live, and that's what God has in mind. So the old man dies and the new man lives—with Christ. The old man died with Christ—that's for real; when Christ died, I died. The new man lives with Christ, because he is raised from the dead and lives in me. Now we live together, and whatever we do, we do it jointly. So I am to *act* on the basis of this truth. "Consider yourself to be dead to sin": negative—and "alive to God": the positive. Romans 6:14, this is the "walk of faith." The first step is *dying* with Christ; the next step is *living* with Christ—in the newness of his resurrection life. A walk is two steps repeated: thus the *walk* of faith. We keep doing this all through life.

"Do not yield your members to sin, yield your members to God" (Rom. 6:13): negative and positive. To cap the whole thing, one little phrase describes it so well, ". . . as men who have been brought from death to life" (Rom. 6:13). That should describe us: "from death to life."

*THE WAY TO GO*

The same thought is captured in 2 Corinthians 4:10, "always carrying in the body the dying of Jesus that the life of Jesus may be manifested in our body." Notice the negative and the positive again. This is to be our *attitude.* This is the way we approach life, a standard operating procedure. In other words, we are not to insist on our own way, to seek to achieve our own personal ambitions and goals; instead we are to let Christ set our ambitions and move under his direction. The dying of Jesus describes what he did in facing into the cross and giving his life; he gave up any plan and ideas of his own in favor of his Father's will. Remember his words in the garden: "Not my will, but thine, Father." Whenever you think of the dying of Jesus, that's what it means. We're to be always carrying this attitude. But the idea is *life* out of death—"that the life of Jesus may be manifested in our body." So the end result is LIFE! Then, 2 Corinthians 4:11 describes the action that *God* is taking, "for we are always being given up to death." This says there is no escaping this process; if you think there is a back door clause, there isn't. God is committed to putting the flesh out of business. So even if we have trouble adopting this attitude, God is going to hem us in anyway. He will put us into the circumstances which constitute "being given up to death," in order that the *life* of Jesus may be shown forth in bodies that are still subject to death. This is the glory of our Christian life; we have bodies that are dying (it's rather obvious to most of us), but in these bodies that are dying, frail and fragile and subject to all the physical and psychological and spiritual ills, God's aim is that the life of Jesus might be shown. This is that treasure-in-earthen-vessels idea from 2 Corinthians 4:7: "But we have this treasure in earthen vessels, to show that the transcendent power belongs to God and not to us." A vessel is just an old pot, but the life of Jesus is that treasure that the pot holds, and that's what God wants to show forth. So here is the theme verse to land on. And notice, we end up on the positive: *the display of the life of God in the Christian.* But in order to accomplish that the old man has to be put to death consistently. Apart from this kind of action we don't act like Christians so we spoil the beauty of God's plan. The illustration on the final page helps us to visualize this action.

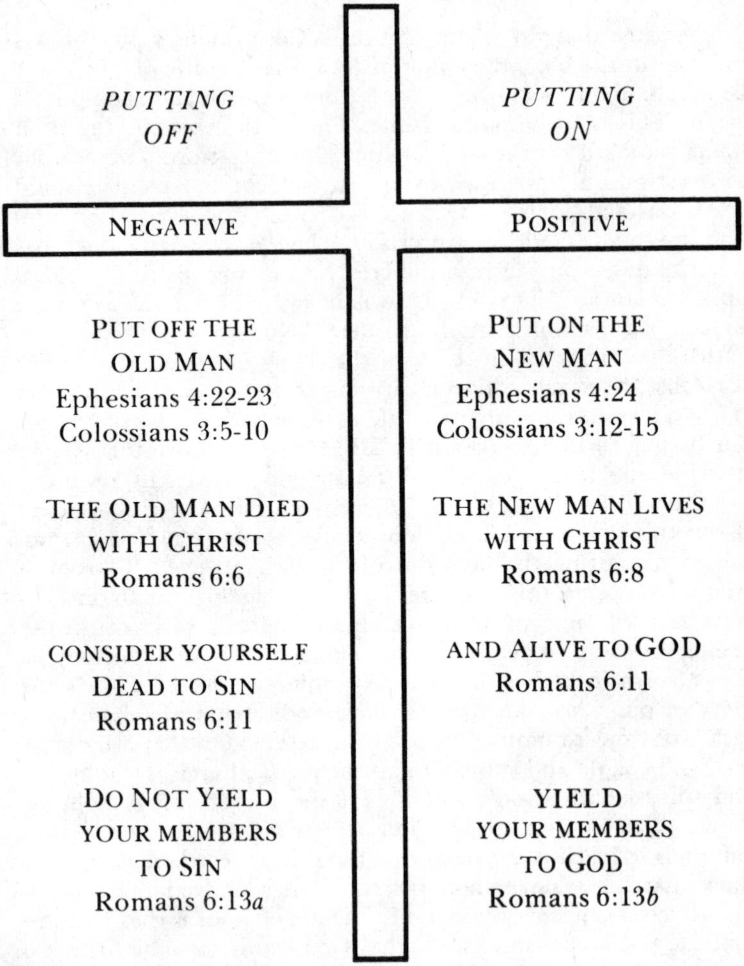

*PUTTING OFF*

NEGATIVE

PUT OFF THE OLD MAN
Ephesians 4:22-23
Colossians 3:5-10

THE OLD MAN DIED WITH CHRIST
Romans 6:6

CONSIDER YOURSELF DEAD TO SIN
Romans 6:11

DO NOT YIELD YOUR MEMBERS TO SIN
Romans 6:13*a*

*PUTTING ON*

POSITIVE

PUT ON THE NEW MAN
Ephesians 4:24
Colossians 3:12-15

THE NEW MAN LIVES WITH CHRIST
Romans 6:8

AND ALIVE TO GOD
Romans 6:11

YIELD YOUR MEMBERS TO GOD
Romans 6:13*b*

AS MEN WHO HAVE BEEN BROUGHT FROM DEATH TO LIFE!
Romans 6:13